WILD ABOUT
OCEANS

WILD ABOUT OCEANS

WRITTEN BY
CAMILLA DE LA BÉDOYÈRE, STEVE PARKER

Little Hippo
Books

First published in 2018 by Miles Kelly Publishing Ltd
Harding's Barn, Bardfield End Green, Thaxted, Essex, CM6 3PX, UK

Copyright © Miles Kelly Publishing Ltd 2018

2 4 6 8 10 9 7 5 3 1

Publishing Director Belinda Gallagher
Creative Director Jo Cowan
Editorial Director Rosie Neave
Senior Editors Amy Johnson, Becky Miles
Cover Designer Joe Jones
Designers Rob Hale, Joe Jones, Andrea Slane
Image Manager Liberty Newton
Indexer Michelle Baker
Production Elizabeth Collins
Reprographics Stephan Davis
Assets Venita Kidwai

All rights reserved. No part of this publication may be reproduced, stored in a retrieval system, or transmitted by any means, electronic, mechanical, photocopying, recording, or otherwise, without the prior permission of the copyright holder.

ISBN 978-1-960009-30-2

Printed in China

Made with paper from a sustainable forest

littlehippobooks.com

Contents

DEEP OCEAN — 6
- The ocean zones — 8
- In deep water — 10
- The Light Zone — 12
- The Twilight Zone — 14
- Monsters of the deep — 16
- The Dark Zone — 18
- The Abyssal Zone — 20
- Glass in the abyss — 22
- The Hadal Zone — 24
- Muds and oozes — 26
- Deep heat — 28
- Deep-sea coral — 30
- On the move — 32
- Breathing and diving — 34
- Glow in the dark — 36
- Deep-sea food — 38
- Anglerfish — 40
- Hide and seek — 42

CORAL REEF — 44
- What are coral reefs? — 46
- Coral animals — 48
- Hard and soft — 50
- Where in the world? — 52
- Types of reef — 54
- Zones of the reef — 56
- Cold water corals — 58
- The Great Barrier Reef — 60
- Caribbean coral — 62
- Islands of fire — 64
- A carnival of color — 66
- On the attack — 68
- Living together — 70
- Night on the reef — 72
- Relying on reefs — 74
- Underwater explorers — 76
- Natural coral killers — 78
- Reefs at risk — 80
- Conserving coral — 82

SEASHORE — 84
- Land meets sea — 86
- Endless battles — 88
- Tides, currents, and winds — 90
- Seashore features — 92
- Coast to coast — 94
- Saltmarshes and mudflats — 96
- Sandy beaches — 98
- Mangrove swamps — 100
- Shingle and pebbles — 102
- Estuaries and lagoons — 104
- Rocky shores and pools — 106
- Visitors to the shore — 108
- Above the seashore — 110
- Skins, shells, and stars — 112
- Seashore dangers — 114
- People and seashores — 116
- Seaside adventures — 118
- Trade and power — 120
- Seashores in trouble? — 122

SHARKS — 124
- Super swimmers — 126
- Shark bodies — 128
- Ultimate killer — 130
- Strange sharks — 132
- Amazing senses — 134
- Hide and seek — 136
- Save our sharks — 138

WHALES AND DOLPHINS — 140
- The greatest animals — 142
- One big family — 144
- Inside whales and dolphins — 146
- Flippers, flukes, and fins — 148
- Sensitive senses — 150
- Clicks, squeaks, and squeals — 152
- Long-distance swimmers — 154

INDEX — 156
ACKNOWLEDGMENTS — 160

DEEP OCEAN

1 Far down in the dark waters of the deep oceans lies a mysterious wilderness. The deep ocean is a place without light, where the water pressure can crush human bones. Until modern times, people did not believe that anything could live here. Now scientists are discovering new creatures all the time, from colossal squid with huge eyes to giant worms that are 6.5 feet in length.

▶ Almost 1.5 miles below the surface of the ocean, an eelpout fish hides among giant tube worms and crabs at a hydrothermal vent. Only two people have been to the deepest part of the oceans, which is about 7 miles below the waves. In contrast, 12 human explorers have walked on the surface of the Moon, which is 238,855 miles from Earth.

The ocean zones

2 **Oceans are enormous areas of water.** They cover more than two-thirds of the Earth's surface. There are five oceans and they make up a giant ecosystem of creatures that depend on seawater to survive.

ARCTIC OCEAN

PACIFIC OCEAN

ATLANTIC OCEAN

SOUTHERN OCEAN

INDIAN OCEAN

LIGHT ZONE 0–650 feet
TWILIGHT ZONE 650–3,300 feet
DARK ZONE 3,300–30,000 feet
ABYSSAL ZONE 2.4–3.7 miles
HADAL ZONE 3.7–6.2 miles

Jellyfish
Sea lily
Tube worms

3 **At their edges, oceans are shallow and teem with life.** These places are called continental shelves. However continental shelves only take up 5 percent of the total area of the oceans. The shelves fall away into deep slopes and from there, the seabed stretches out as dark, enormous plains.

◄▲ There are five oceans. They are all connected and make up one giant mass of water.

▶ Scientists divide the ocean into five layers, or zones. Different types of animals live in the different zones.

DELIGHT IN LIGHT
Find out about the wavelengths of white light. How many colors make up white light, and what are they? Find the answers by searching on the Internet with the keywords "rainbow" and "light."

DEEP OCEAN

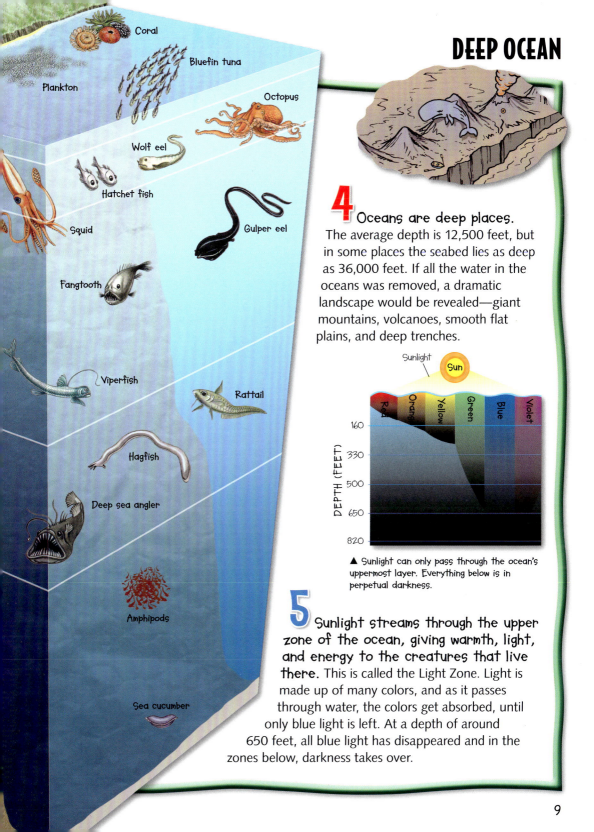

4 **Oceans are deep places.** The average depth is 12,500 feet, but in some places the seabed lies as deep as 36,000 feet. If all the water in the oceans was removed, a dramatic landscape would be revealed—giant mountains, volcanoes, smooth flat plains, and deep trenches.

▲ Sunlight can only pass through the ocean's uppermost layer. Everything below is in perpetual darkness.

5 **Sunlight streams through the upper zone of the ocean, giving warmth, light, and energy to the creatures that live there.** This is called the Light Zone. Light is made up of many colors, and as it passes through water, the colors get absorbed, until only blue light is left. At a depth of around 650 feet, all blue light has disappeared and in the zones below, darkness takes over.

9

In deep water

6 **Living in water is nothing like living in air.** The ocean is one of Earth's most remarkable habitats. Ocean water is constantly moving and changing. The creatures that live here have to cope without light, and the weight of many tons of water above them.

8 **As you travel deeper into the ocean you will feel a great weight on your body.** Water is 830 times denser than air, and it is very heavy. It is water's density that helps things to float, or stay buoyant. However, the further down you go, the more pressure the water forces on you.

◀ Cold water is denser than warm water, and it sinks to the ocean depths near the polar regions.

◀ Water travels in currents around the world. The largest and deepest of these form a system called the global conveyor.

▶ Water pressure is measured in atmospheres (atm). Pressure increases with depth, squashing the molecules of air in this balloon.

7 **At the surface, wind creates waves and the Moon's gravitational pull causes tides.** Further down, other forces are in action. Ocean water is continually moving, passing around the globe in giant streams called currents. If you were to get caught in one of these strong, deep currents, after 1,000 years you would have journeyed all around the world!

DEEP OCEAN

9 **Although you will soon be cold, you may notice that the temperature of the water around you doesn't change much.** Ocean water has great heat capacity, which means that it warms up slowly and cools down slowly too. It can hold on to its temperature about 4,000 times better than air can.

▼ Many enormous animals, such as this basking shark, live in the ocean. The dense, salty seawater supports their great weight.

10 **The good news is that you won't have to work hard to get food.** If you stay still, it will float right past your nose. Because water is dense, tiny creatures and particles of food are suspended in it. Some sea creatures can wave tentacles to catch food, or just open their mouths as they swim!

◄ A magnified view of plankton, tiny animals and plants that float or swim in seawater. They often become food for bigger animals.

MAKING WATER HEAVY

You will need:
two identical cups containing the same amount of water   salt

Add salt to one of the cups and stir. Continue until no more salt will dissolve. Weigh both cups—the salty one should be heavier. Salty water is denser and heavier than fresh water.

11 **You should never drink seawater.** It has lots of minerals, called salts, dissolved in it. A single bath of seawater contains 6 pounds of salts. Most of that is sodium chloride (common salt). Gases, such as oxygen and nitrogen are also dissolved in seawater.

Other elements 0.6%
Sodium 1%
Chloride 1.9%
Water 96.5%
Salt 3.5%

► A beaker of ocean water may look dirty, but it is full of substances that are food for tiny organisms called phytoplankton.

The Light Zone

12 The top 650 feet of the ocean is called the Light Zone. At the continental shelf, sunlight can reach all the way to the seabed. However within 30 feet of the water's surface, nearly all of the red parts of light have been absorbed, which means that many creatures appear dull in color.

▲ The shiny scales on tuna fish reflect sunlight as they dart from side to side, to confuse their predators.

▶ Green turtles have to visit the surface to breathe air, then they dive to feed on marine plants.

13 Sunlight provides the energy for plants to grow. Marine plants such as seaweed need light in order to make food from carbon dioxide and water, in a process called photosynthesis. Plants also produce oxygen, the gas we breathe, and without it there would be no life in the oceans.

◀ Marine plants, including seaweed (shown here) and phytoplankton, are called algae.

DEEP OCOAN

◀ Emperor penguins can stay underwater for up to 20 minutes at a time, hunting for fish.

14 Many marine plants are almost invisible. They are called phytoplankton and are so tiny that they have to be viewed with a microscope. Phytoplankton begin a food web that supports nearly all ocean life. They are eaten by microscopic animals, called zooplankton, and bigger animals too.

15 The Light Zone is bright and full of food, making it a busy habitat. Fish such as anchovies and sardines come to feed on swarms of plankton. In turn larger animals, such as sharks, come to prey upon the fish. Even birds, such as pelicans and penguins, enter this habitat to grab what food they can.

16 More than six billion tons of phytoplankton grow in the Light Zone every year and they produce half of the oxygen in our atmosphere. Without them there would be almost no animal life in the oceans, and few animals on land either.

17 Most swimming animals of the Light Zone can move into deeper water to escape from predators. At around a depth of 650 feet almost all sunlight has been absorbed and darkness takes over in the Twilight Zone.

▼ Warm-water corals need sunlight to grow, and they build reefs in the Light Zone.

The Twilight Zone

TWILIGHT ZONE

18 From a depth of 650 to 3,300 feet lies the Twilight Zone. Just enough light reaches this zone for animals to see, and be seen by. Predators and prey battle it out in a constant fight for survival.

19 Mighty sperm whales plunge into the Twilight Zone when they are hunting squid. They can dive to depths of 3,300 feet and hold their breath for up to 90 minutes at a time. The deepest known dive of any sperm whale was 9,800 feet, and the whale swam at a speed of 13 feet per second to get there!

▲ A nautilus fills the chambers in its shell with water or gas by a tube called a siphuncle. Like octopuses and squid, a nautilus propels itself by pushing water out of its funnel.

20 The nautilus can swim, float, and move up and down in the Twilight Zone. It lives in the outermost chamber of its shell, and its inner chambers are filled with gas or liquid. By pushing gas into the chambers, liquid is forced out and the nautilus becomes lighter—and floats up. When the gas is replaced with liquid, the nautilus sinks.

◄ Huge sperm whales are mammals, which means they have to return to the surface to breathe.

21 **It is hard to see if your eyes are deep inside your head.** Barreleye fish don't mind because they have see-through heads. They swim with their big, green eyes peering upward. When the fish sees its prey, it flips its body upright and rotates its eyes in its head. This allows the fish to keep its prey in view while swimming up to grab it.

Eye
Mouth
Nostril

◄ A barreleye fish's eyes are very sensitive, which help it to spot its prey in low light.

▼ Comb jellies swim by beating rows of comblike plates, which bend light rays to make colorful shimmers.

22 **There are few hard surfaces to attach to, so animals in the Twilight Zone are mostly floaters and swimmers.** Many have unusual shapes and their bodies are often soft and watery. Comb jellies are soft-bodied animals, but they can turn hard by contracting muscles. Some have long, sticky tentacles to grab prey.

▼ Sea pens anchor themselves to the seafloor in the Twilight Zone. They feed on plankton by catching it in their feathery branches.

TRUE OR FALSE?
1. Barreleye fish have see-through heads.
2. Sperm whales can breathe underwater.
3. Nautiluses swim using fins.
4. The Twilight Zone is pitch black.

Answers:
1. True 2. False 3. False 4. False

Monsters of the deep

23 **Giant squid are monsters of the deep.** They can grow to 50 feet in length, including tentacles, which alone can grow to 40 feet. Their eyes are thought to be the largest of any animal. Each one is up to 16 inches in diameter!

24 Little is known about these mysterious animals because they live in the Twilight Zone. Giant squid can swim well, and with their good eyesight they can spot fishing nets and move swiftly away. Very few have ever been caught, and what is known about them has been revealed from dead specimens, or remains that have been found in the stomachs of sperm whales.

▶ Giant squid have a reputation as fearsome monsters. In fact, they are more likely to be gentle giants of the deep.

ANIMAL GIANTS

Put these animal giants in order of size, from largest to smallest:
African elephant
Hercules beetle
Blue whale   Giant squid

Answer:
Blue whale, giant squid, African elephant, Hercules beetle

Teeth   Sucker   Tentacle

25 **People have known about giant squid for hundreds of years.** The first one to be recorded was found in Iceland in 1639, and the stories and myths began. People feared that these creatures could sink ships or grab people on deck. When sperm whales were discovered with scars caused by giant squid suckers, people realized that these predators battle with large whales.

26 **Giant squid are predators.** No one knows for sure how they live, but like other squid they probably hunt fish, octopuses, and smaller squid. Their muscular tentacles are equipped with giant, toothed suckers that can grab hold of wriggly prey.

▶ The eye of a giant squid has a diameter bigger than a person's head.

The Dark Zone

27 Below 3,300 feet absolutely no light can penetrate. So far from the Sun's rays, this habitat is intensely cold, and there is bone-crushing pressure from the enormous weight of water above. It is called the Dark Zone, and it extends to 2.5 miles below the ocean's surface.

28 It snows in the Dark Zone! Billions of particles fall down toward the seabed, and this is called marine snow. This "snow" is made up of droppings from animals above, and animals and plants that have died. Small flakes often collect together to become larger and heavier, drifting down up to 650 feet a day. Marine snow is an important source of food for billions of deep-sea creatures.

▲ Fierce-looking fangtooth fish can swim to depths of around 3 miles, into the Abyssal Zone, when they follow their prey.

29 The orange roughy lives in deep water where its color appears black if any light reaches it. This is believed to be one of the longest living fish—one individual allegedly reached 149 years of age.

30 A fangtooth fish may have enormous teeth, but at only 6 inches in length, these fish are not as scary as they sound. Fangtooths have poor eyesight, and in the Dark Zone other senses are just as valuable. These fish can detect tiny movements in the surrounding water, which they follow to find their prey.

DEEP OCEAN

31 **Greenland sharks live under the Arctic ice at depths of up to 6,500 feet.** Not much is known about how these giant fish live because of their unusual habitat. Nearly all Greenland sharks are blind because of parasites, tiny creatures that damage their eyes. However they have a good sense of smell, which they use to sniff out the rotting flesh of other dead animals to eat. They also prey on seals and other sharks.

▲ Greenland sharks can grow to 20 feet long. They live in the Arctic and often swim close to shore, but pose little threat to humans.

▼ Giant isopods are crustaceans that live in the Dark Zone. They are related to crabs, shrimps, lobsters, and woodlice, and can reach a length of 14 inches. Isopods have long antennae that help them feel their way in the dark.

32 **Giant isopods are peculiar crawling creatures that look like huge woodlice.** Their bodies are protected by tough plates, and they can roll themselves up into a ball when they come under attack. Isopods live on the seabed, searching for soft-bodied animals to eat.

The Abyssal Zone

▼ The Abyssal Zone is an enormous seascape of mountains, volcanoes, trenches, and muddy plains.

33 Below the Dark Zone is the Abyssal Zone, or abyss, which reaches from 2.5 to 3.7 miles. Where the continental slope ends, the sea floor stretches out in a giant plain. Around one third of the seabed is in the Abyssal Zone.

34 The abyssal plains have mountains (called sea mounts), trenches and valleys. Many sea mounts are drowned volcanoes, and there may be 30,000 of them in the world's oceans. The sides of the mounts are sheer, which causes water to flow upward in a process called upwelling. This flow of water brings nutrients to the area, and many animals live in these habitats.

35 Most waters of the Abyssal Zone contain little food. Animals rely on finding marine snow, which may take several months to fall from the surface, or hunting other deep-sea creatures. Many are scavengers, which means they only feed when they find food, such as the remains of other animals that have died. With a shortage of food, creatures here move around very little to save energy.

◄ Basket stars can survive in the abyss. Each arm is branched into many smaller parts to catch particles of marine snow.

DEEP OCEAN

▼ There are around 60 types of hagfish. They have eellike bodies with four hearts, but no bones.

37 Sea cucumbers, also known as sea pigs, are sausagelike animals of the abyss. They are enjoyed as a tasty delicacy in some parts of the world.

36 An Atlantic hagfish is a slimy, fishlike animal of the abyss with disgusting eating habits. It is nearly blind but has a good sense of smell, which helps it to find prey. A hagfish has tentacles and hooks around its mouth to grab hold of its victim's flesh. Then it burrows into the prey's body, eating its insides. A hagfish can survive for many months without feeding again.

38 The most common fish in the Abyssal Zone are called rattails, or grenadiers. There are around 300 different types of rattails in the world and scientists estimate that there are at least 20 billion of just one type—that's more than three times the number of humans!

▼ Rattails are slow movers so they probably creep up on their prey to catch them. They are also scavengers, eating anything they can find on the seabed. Here, they swarm around a bait cage and the submersible *Mir I*.

Glass in the abyss

39 **One of the world's strongest types of glass is made by a creature of the abyss.** The Venus' flower basket is a type of glass sponge that has a strong skeleton. Glass sponges build their structures from strands of silica, the material used to make glass.

▶ The Venus' flower basket lives at depths of 3 miles in the ocean waters of Southeast Asia.

40 **Sponges are the simplest of all animals.** Most sponges live in oceans and they are attached to solid surfaces. Since they can't move to find food, sponges create water currents that move through their bodies so they can filter out any particles of food.

Osculum
Flow of water
Spicules (strands of silica)
Pore

▶ Special cells near the pores have taillike parts, that move in a beating motion. This sucks water into the sponge, and out through the osculum.

◀ The Venus' flower basket is strong because it has a lattice structure. The Eiffel Tower in France has a similar structure.

41 **Sponges don't have normal body parts, tissues, or organs.** They are more like an organized collection of cells. Their bodies lack bones, so they are supported by a structure made from tough materials, such as silica. Engineers examine creatures and plants that build tough structures to help them design better buildings.

43 **The Venus' flower basket glows with bright colors around its base.** In the darkness, the lights and colors may attract tiny, curious creatures, which are swept into the sponge by water currents and eaten.

42 **The Venus' flower basket builds its structure by "gluing" together needles of silica, each no thicker than a human hair.** The construction follows a beautiful pattern, which gives the sponge great strength to withstand the water pressure at depths of 3 miles or more.

▶ Cloud sponges are another type of deep-living glass sponge. They can provide a safe living area for other small animals.

The Hadal Zone

44 The oceans plunge to depths greater than 3.7 miles in only a few places, called trenches. This is called the Hadal Zone, named after the Greek word "hades," which means "unseen." It's the perfect name for the most mysterious habitat on Earth.

▲ Earth's largest mountain, Everest, could fit into eight of the world's deepest trenches.

45 The deepest of all trenches is the Mariana Trench in the Pacific Ocean, which plunges to 36,200 feet. It is 1,584 miles long and about 43 miles wide. This trench was created when two massive plates in the Earth's crust collided millions of years ago.

46 Scientists know very little about animals that live in the Hadal Zone. Collecting live animals from this depth causes great problems because their bodies are suited to high water pressure. When they are brought to the surface the pressure drops, and they die.

▶ Snailfish thrive in the ocean's deepest waters and have been found at depths of more than 23,000 feet. They have large heads and bodies that taper to slender tails.

DEEP OCEAN

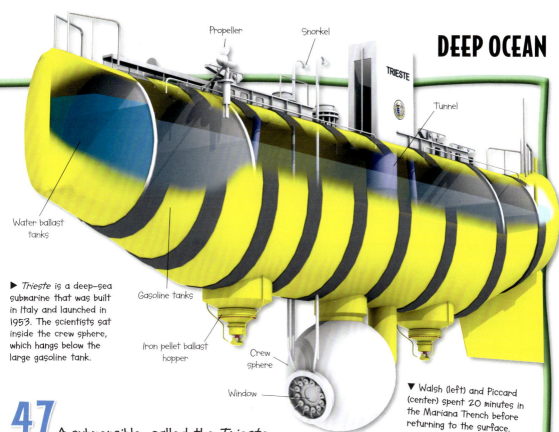

▶ *Trieste* is a deep-sea submarine that was built in Italy and launched in 1953. The scientists sat inside the crew sphere, which hangs below the large gasoline tank.

▼ Walsh (left) and Piccard (center) spent 20 minutes in the Mariana Trench before returning to the surface.

47 A submersible, called the *Trieste*, was built in the 1950s, which could dive to the Hadal Zone. In 1960, explorers Don Walsh and Jacques Piccard climbed aboard and began one of the most dangerous journeys ever undertaken. It took five hours to descend to 35,797 feet in the Mariana Trench and here they saw the deepest-known crustacean—a red shrimp. Other similar creatures called amphipods have been collected at depths of 34,500 feet.

CURIOUS CREATURES

Draw a picture of your own Hadal Zone creature. It should probably be dark-colored, with tiny eyes, or none at all, and very ugly. Body parts that help it feel its way around a dark habitat would be helpful.

48 The deepest-living fish are believed to belong to a family called *Abyssobrotula*. One fish, *Abyssobrotula galatheae*, was captured in 1970 at a depth of 27,460 feet. It was found by explorers in the Puerto Rico Trench. Scientists tried to bring the fish to the surface, but it did not survive the journey.

Muds and oozes

49 The remains of all marine creatures eventually get eaten or drift down to the seabed. These remains, which are mostly marine snow, become deep-sea sediments. They form layers of muddy ooze that can be up to 1,500 feet thick.

50 Most creatures that live on the seafloor are scavengers. A dead whale can provide food for millions of other animals, including shrimplike amphipods and copepods, worms, rattails, and hagfish.

Greenland shark
Amphipods
Rattails
Hagfish

KEY
① Crabs, hagfish, amphipods, rattails, and sharks strip the flesh from the fresh body.
② Next, worms are the main colonizers, living off the enriched sediments.
③ Finally, the whale's bones produce sulfides—chemicals that bacteria, mussels, and clams feast on.

51 The muddy layer of the abyssal plain may look smooth, but close up there are tiny trails and holes. Every handful of mud contains millions of microscopic animals. Foraminifera and radiolarians are tiny shelled single-celled organisms that live in the sediments. When they die, their shells dissolve into the muddy ooze.

DEEP OCEAN

52 The abyssal plains are home to many types of sea cucumbers. These sausage-shaped animals are common in this habitat. Some burrow in the mud, while others can swim. Most move over the seafloor, picking up any bits of food they can find.

53 The seabed of the Antarctic Ocean has some megasized animals. Scientists found giant spiders and worms, and fish with huge eyes and body parts that scientists described as "dangly bits!"

◀ It can take up to 100 years for a whale carcass to be devoured. More than 30,000 different types of animal feed and live off the carcass at different stages.

▼ Tripod fish stand still for hours at a time, facing the water currents, and wait for food to drift toward them.

54 Tripod fish have very long spines, called rays, on their fins. They use these to stand on the muddy seabed without sinking as they wait for prey to drift by. They are almost blind but can sense vibrations made by other animals nearby.

Deep heat

55 The deep ocean floor is mainly a cold place, where animals struggle to survive. However, there are some extraordinary areas where the water is heated to temperatures of 750°F and living things thrive.

▼ The minerals in the water produce dark clouds that look like smoke, and these vents are called "black smokers." Over time, they build up rocky structures called chimneys, which can grow to the height of a 15-story building.

56 Below the Earth's surface is a layer of hot, semiliquid rock, called **magma**. In places, magma is close to the ocean floor. Water seeps into cracks in rocks, called hydrothermal vents, and is heated. The water dissolves minerals from the rocks as it travels up toward the ocean floor, and bursts through a vent like a fountain.

57 The first hydrothermal vents were discovered in the Pacific Ocean in the 1970s. Since then, others have been found in the Atlantic, Indian, and Arctic Oceans. The largest known region of hydrothermal vents lies near the Mid-Atlantic Ridge and is the size of a soccer pitch.

KEY
1. Vent mussel
2. Ratfish
3. Vent crab
4. Vent octopus
5. Chimney
6. Sea spider
7. Tube worms

DEEP OCEAN

58 Some hydrothermal vents do not support much life, other than microscopic creatures. Others support colonies of limpets, shrimps, starfish, and tube worms, which survive without any sunlight. They are able to live and grow due to the minerals in the superheated water from the vents.

▲ Hydrothermal vents known as "white smokers" release cooler water and plumes of different minerals to black smokers.

59 Vent tube worms can grow to 6 feet long and they live without eating anything. Each worm is attached to the seabed and is protected by the tube it lives in. A red plume at the top collects seawater, which is rich in minerals. These minerals are passed to bacteria in the worm's body, and are then turned into nutrients.

◄ Bacteria that live inside the tube worm turn the minerals into food, which the worm needs to survive.

- Plume
- Blood vessel
- Heart
- Bacteria
- Tube

UNDER PRESSURE

You will need:
milk carton   sticky tape

With an adult's help, make four holes on one side of an old milk carton, one above the other. Put sticky tape over the holes and fill the carton with water. Hold it over a bowl while you pull the tape off. Water will pour out fastest from the bottom hole because it has the most pressure on it.

Deep-sea coral

60 Tiny creatures called coral polyps build large reefs in the cold, deep ocean. Coral reefs are often found in warm, shallow waters, and they attract a wide variety of life. Cold-water reefs are less varied habitats, but there may be more cold-water reefs than warm-water ones.

62 Coral polyps have tube-shaped bodies and tentacles around their mouths. All polyps feed by filtering food particles from the water, and they have thousands of tiny stingers to stun bigger prey.

61 Air pollution from carbon dioxide causes the oceans to become more acidic. This stops polyps, especially cold-water ones, from being able to grow their stony skeletons.

63 Coral polyps produce a hard substance called calcium carbonate, which forms a protective cup around them. Over time, the stony cups collect and grow into a reef, held together by a cement of sand, mud, and other particles.

Bubble gum coral

Flytrap anemone

Lophelia pertusa

Squat lobster

DEEP OCEAN

▲ A specimen of bamboo coral is carefully lifted from the deep sea in a collection box that is attached to a submersible.

▼ Cold-water coral creates a special habitat where other animals can live, find food, and shelter. A group of living things that depend on one habitat like this is called an ecosystem.

64 A type of cold-water coral polyp called Lophelia is the most common reef builder in the Atlantic Ocean. One reef can cover 21,500 square feet and is home to animals such as squat lobsters, long-legged crabs, and fish—especially babies called larvae.

65 Other cold-water communities have been found in the deep oceans. Engineers drilling for oil in the Gulf of Mexico found cold seeps (places where gases leak out of cracks in the rocks) and animal life thrived nearby. The gases are an energy source for bacteria that feed there. Animals that feed on the bacteria are in turn eaten by crabs, corals, worms, and fish.

Brittle stars

Alfonsino fish

Gorgonian sea fan

On the move

66 Traveling in the ocean is different from traveling in air. Animals can simply float or drift along because they weigh 50 times less in water than they do in air. Currents help too. They can bring food to animals that are attached to the seabed, or they can carry animals toward food.

◀ Little sea butterflies are a type of sea snail. They can swim slowly through the water by flapping their "wings," or they float in the currents.

▼ For this tube anemone, being attached to the seabed means it is impossible to make a quick getaway from the giant nudibranch that is attacking it (bottom).

67 Animals caught in deep-sea currents have to go with the flow, unless they are strong swimmers. Swimming takes 830 times as much energy as staying still because water is dense and heavy. Tiny zooplankton are weak swimmers, so when they get caught in currents, they drift along until they become free.

68 Many marine animals cannot move from one place to another. They are attached to the seabed and stay there, waiting for food to come to them. These animals, such as sea lilies and tube anemones, have feathery tentacles that they use to filter the seawater and collect particles of food.

DEEP OCEAN

69 **Billions of animals undertake a journey every night.** They travel up from the Twilight and Dark Zones into the Light Zone to feed, and return to deeper water in the morning. This mass movement is called a vertical migration and it represents the largest migration, or animal journey, on Earth.

70 **Lantern fish are mighty movers of the ocean.** The champion is called *Ceratoscopelus warmingii* and it lives at a depth of 5,900 feet in the day. At night it swims upward to depths of 330 feet to feed and avoid predators, and then it swims back. This feat is like a person running three marathons in a day!

DAY

Albatross
Phytoplankton
100 feet
Mackerel
Copepods
Comb jellies
Jellyfish
650 feet
Blue shark
Squid
Sperm whale
Lantern fish
330 feet

NIGHT

Albatross
Mackerel
Phytoplankton
Comb jellies
Copepods
Lantern fish
Jellyfish
Squid
Blue shark
Sperm whale

◀▲ About half of all marine creatures move upward at night toward the Light Zone where there is plenty of food. They descend to lower depths when the sun rises.

Breathing and diving

Gill slits

▲ As a shark swims, water enters its mouth, passes over its gills where oxygen is absorbed, and then leaves through the gill slits.

71 Animals need to take a gas called oxygen into their bodies to release energy from food. Taking in oxygen is called breathing, and the process of using it to release energy is called respiration. Most marine animals are specially adapted to take in dissolved oxygen from seawater.

SPEED DEMONS!
Blow up a balloon. It is now filled with gas, like a swim bladder. Put the balloon in a bowl or bath of water and try to make it sink. Now fill the balloon with water, and see if it will float.

72 Fish breathe using gills. Like our lungs take oxygen from air, gills take in oxygen from water. Most fish also have a swim bladder, which helps them to cope with the changing pressure as they swim deeper. A swim bladder is a gas-filled sac that expands as a fish moves upward, and shrinks as it descends. All deep-sea fish have gills, but they do not have swim bladders because the immense pressure would crush them.

Blowhole

◄ Whales, such as this killer whale, come to the surface to breathe. They have one or two blowholes on the top of their heads. These are like nostrils, and this is where air enters the body. When air is breathed out of a blowhole it creates a water spout.

DEEP OCEAN

As a sperm whale dives, its ribs and lungs contract (shrink). They expand again when the whale surfaces.

The whale's heartbeat slows by half so less oxygen is needed.

The spermaceti organ is a huge mass of oil. It probably helps the whale to dive deep by changing its ability to float.

The nasal passages fill with cool water to help the whale sink.

▲ The sperm whale is adapted for diving in very deep water. It can stay underwater for up to 90 minutes while hunting for giant squid.

73 Seals, dolphins, and whales are air-breathing mammals, but their bodies are adapted to life in water. The sperm whale can store oxygen in its blood and muscles, which allows it to descend to over 3,300 feet to hunt. Its flexible ribcage allows the whale's lungs to shrink during a dive.

74 Super-speedy pilot whales are called "cheetahs of the deep." During the day, these predators swim at depths of around 1,000 feet, but at night they plunge to 3,300 feet in search of prey. Pilot whales can plummet 30 feet a second at top swimming speed. They need to be fast to catch their prey of large squid, but also because they need to get back to the surface to breathe.

▼ Most marine worms have feathery gills that absorb oxygen from the water. However, some do not have gills and absorb oxygen through their skin.

75 Simple creatures do not have special body parts for breathing. They can absorb oxygen from the water directly through their skins. The amount of oxygen in the water falls from the surface to a depth of around 3,300 feet, but it increases again at greater depths.

Glow in the dark

76 Animals of the deep create their own light to attract prey, a mate or to confuse predators. This is called bioluminescence and it takes place in organs called photophores. These usually produce blue light, but some animals can glow with green, red or yellow light.

Bioluminescent lure used to attract prey

◀ A shortnose greeneye fish produces its own light. In the dark, it glows green, especially its eyes.

Under white light

In the dark

▶ The special cells inside a photophore that produce light are called photocytes.

Light rays
Skin
Lens
Color filter
Photocytes (light-producing cells)
Reflector

◀ The viperfish has rows of photophores along its underside. These help to hide it from predators below.

77 Hatchet fish are deceivers of the Twilight Zone. Photophores on their bellies produce light and disguise the fishes' outlines when seen from below, against the faint light. Hatchet fish can also adjust the light to match the brightness of any light from above.

DEEP OCEAN

78 **Spotted lantern fish use their photophores to attract mates.** They are one of the brightest deep-sea fish, with brilliant displays of bioluminescence along their sides and bellies. The photophores are arranged in different patterns depending on whether the fish is male or female, and what type of lantern fish it is. This helps the fish to find the right mate.

79 **It is not just fish that can glow in the dark.** Mauve stinger jellyfish emit a beautiful violet-blue color when they are disturbed. Firefly squid not only cover their bodies with lights, they can also produce a cloud of glowing particles that distracts predators while they make a quick getaway.

▶ Mauve stinger jellyfish produce quick flashes of light when they sense movement in the water. They even flash when waves pass over them at the ocean's surface.

80 **Tiny vampire squid have enormous eyes and can produce light all over their bodies whenever they want to.** These squid are able to control their bioluminescence, producing dazzling displays of patterned light that can be dimmed or brightened, probably to scare off predators. When a vampire squid is hunting it does not light up. This means it can surprise its prey.

BIG WORD, LITTLE WORD
Use the word "bioluminescence" to create as many new words as you can by rearranging the letters. Each word must be at least two letters long. Use a dictionary to check the spelling of your words.

Deep-sea food

81 **The ocean food chain begins in the Light Zone.** Phytoplankton use the Sun's energy to grow. In turn, they are eaten by other creatures, passing on energy and nutrients. It takes a long time for energy and nutrients to filter down to the seafloor, so many deep-sea animals scavenge food, eating whatever they find, while others hunt.

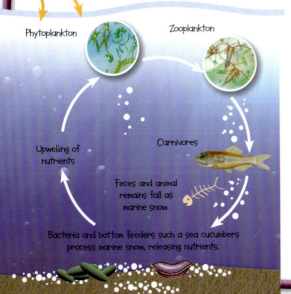

▼ Nearly all energy used by marine life comes from the Light Zone. Phytoplankton begin the nutrient cycle, and upward-flowing water currents complete it by bringing nutrients back to the surface.

82 **Copepods and krill (zooplankton) may be small but they play a big role in the deep-ocean ecosystem.** These tiny, plant-eating crustaceans exist in their billions. They swim up to the surface every evening to try to avoid being eaten. In the morning they swim back down into the deep, dark waters. Krill can live to depths of 6,500 feet.

83 **One krill is not much bigger than a paperclip.** But the total weight of all the krill in the world is greater than the total weight of all the people on the planet!

DEEP OCEAN

◀ Goblin sharks have soft, flabby bodies and long, strange-looking snouts. They are pinkish white in color.

85 Fangtooth fish are also known as ogrefish. They use their unusually sharp, long teeth to grab hold of squid and fish. Food is scarce in the deep ocean, but with such large jaws, fangtooths attempt to eat almost any prey that comes along, even animals that are larger than themselves.

84 Large predators, such as sharks, seals, and whales, may reach the Dark Zone, but few go deeper. Goblin sharks swim slowly in the Dark Zone and they have snouts that may help them to find food. Their huge jaws can snap forward to grab prey such as small fish and squid.

▼ Gulper eels can grown to 6 feet in length. They have pink photophores on their tails to attract prey.

▶ This soft-bodied animal called a predatory tunicate lives in the Twilight Zone. When an animal swims into its hoodlike mouth it closes shut like a Venus flytrap.

86 Gulper eels are all mouth. These predators of the Dark Zone have enormous mouths, but small teeth. It may be that gulper eels use their big mouths for catching lots of small prey at a time, rather than one large, meaty prey.

Anglerfish

87 **If you cannot find food in the dark, make it come to you!** Anglerfish have long growths on their heads that work like fishing rods, and the tips are coated in glowing bacteria. Other animals are attracted to the glowing light, called a lure, and are quickly snapped up by the anglerfish.

88 **Pacific blackdragons are dark on the outside, and the inside!** Their stomachs are black so when they swallow fish that glow, the light doesn't show and encourage predators to approach!

▲ In the 2003 Disney Pixar movie *Finding Nemo*, Marlin and Dory narrowly escape the jaws of an anglerfish.

89 **There are many different types of anglerfish and all look very strange.** The hairy anglerfish is one of the strangest and it lives at depths of up to 4,900 feet. It gets its name from its fins, which have long spikes, and the sensitive hairs that cover its body.

Tassel-chinned angler

Long-rod angler

Deep-sea angler

DEEP OCEAN

Males

▶ Two tiny males are attached to this female Regan's anglerfish. These anglerfish are sometimes called phantom anglerfish.

90 **Finding a mate in the dark can be tough, so some male anglerfish stay attached to a female!** The males are much smaller than the females, so they can grab hold and hitch a lift that lasts for life. While scientists have found many types of female anglerfish, they are still searching for some of their tiny male relations!

91 **A dragonfish also lures prey to its death.** When a dragonfish spies a shrimp to eat it produces a red spotlight made by photophores below its eyes. The shrimp can't see red, so it is unaware it is being hunted. The dragonfish then snaps up its prey in its large mouth, full of ultra-sharp teeth.

▼ Monkfish are so well camouflaged that they are almost impossible to spot when lying on the ocean floor.

92 **Anglers are types of anglerfish that lie on the seafloor.** Their wide, flat bodies are covered in soft, fleshy growths that help them to blend in with the mud where they hide. Anglers use their fins to shuffle along, flicking their lures as they go. They are often caught and sold as food, and also better known as monkfish.

Hide and seek

93 Throughout the animal kingdom, creatures use colors and patterns to hide from predators or prey. In the deep oceans, colors appear different because of the way light is absorbed by water. Colors, other than black and red, are not very useful for camouflage. Deep-sea creatures have developed special ways to avoid being detected.

▲ Deep-sea glass squid are mostly transparent, apart from some brightly colored polka dots on their bodies.

94 Some deep-sea animals are well adapted for hiding and seeking. Glass squid are almost completely transparent, so light passes through their bodies, helping them go unnoticed. A thin body can help too, because it is hard to see from certain angles. With little light around, enormous eyes are useful. Big eyes can collect more light and turn it into hazy images.

▲ Spookfish have enormous eyes, giving them very good vision.

DEEP OCEAN

95 Silvery scales on a fish's back are perfect for reflecting light and confusing a predator. When shimmering scales are seen against dim rays of light in the Twilight Zone, the outline of a fish's body becomes less obvious, and it fades into the background or even disappears.

96 When there is no light, animals rely on senses other than sight. Many deep-sea animals can feel vibrations in the water. Shrimp have sensory organs all over their bodies, including their antennae, which can detect movements nearby. Many fish can also sense the small electrical fields generated by other living things.

▲ By using their photophores to produce light and their silvery scales to reflect light, hatchet fish become almost invisible to predators.

Silvery, reflective scales

Light-producing photophores

▶ The snipe eel's jaws curve away from each other so they never fully close.

97 Snipe eels have long, ribbonlike bodies, and jaws that look like a bird's bill. They live at depths of up to 5,900 feet and can grow to 5 feet in length. As males mature their jaws shrink, but their nostrils grow longer. This probably improves their sense of smell and helps them to find females.

ODD ONE OUT

Which of these animals uses color and pattern to scare other animals, rather than to hide?

Zebra   Wasp   Tiger
Leaf insect
Arctic fox

Answer: Wasp

CORAL REEF

98 Beautiful coral reefs lie beneath the sparkling surfaces of sapphire-blue seas. Although they only take up a tiny amount of space in the world's oceans, coral reefs contain more than one-quarter of all types of sea creatures and are home to billions of animals and plants. Coral reefs are among the Earth's most precious places but they are in grave danger of disappearing forever.

◀ Reefs teem with life as fish dart and dash around stonelike coral structures. Panda butterflyfish inhabit reefs in tropical oceans and can grow up to 8 inches in length.

What are coral reefs?

99 Coral reefs are ocean habitats (homes) made by the creatures that live inside them. Tiny coral animals called polyps live together in huge numbers, known as colonies. They can grow for thousands of years, building reefs that can measure more than 1,200 miles long.

▲ The coral reefs in the Florida Keys National Marine Sanctuary are so vast they can be seen from space.

100 Reefs are home to many animals and plants. Together, the reef and all the things living in it make up an ecosystem. Coral reefs are some of the most varied ecosystems in the world, and are thriving, colorful places that burst with life.

◀ Sea anemones attach themselves to the reef structure and fish hide away in the many nooks and crannies.

CORAL REEF KEY
① White-spotted rose anemone
② Club-tipped anemone
③ Gopher rockfish

TRUE OR FALSE?

1. Coral reefs grow best in dirty water.
2. A group of polyps living together is called a herd.
3. Mangrove tree roots only grow on land.
4. Coral reefs have been around for 230 years.

Answers:
All are false.

101 It is not only coral polyps that help a reef to grow. Polyps provide the framework of a reef, but other living things add to the structure. Some marine (sea) organisms, such as sponges and sea cucumbers, have a hard substance called silicon in their skeletons. When they die, their skeletons add to the coral reef.

102 Land-living animals and plants also depend on reefs. In shallow water, plants take root in the mud and sand that collect around a reef. Mangrove trees and sea grasses grow here—the spaces around their roots make good places for animals, such as crabs, to hide. Long-legged birds also wade through mud and water, looking for food.

103 Coral reefs have been around for at least 230 million years. They are among the oldest ecosystems in the world. Despite their great age, coral reefs do not appear to have changed very much in this time.

◀ The warm waters around mangrove roots are a perfect place for soft tree corals to grow.

Coral animals

104 Coral polyps are the little animals that build reefs. Their soft bodies are like rubber tubes with an opening at their center. This is the mouth, which is surrounded by rows of tentacles. Each tentacle is equipped with stingers called cnidocytes (say nido-sites).

QUIZ
These coral words have been jumbled up. Can you unscramble the letters to make sense of them?

1. LOPPY 2. LACETENT
3. AGALE 4. LORAC

Answers:
1. Polyp 2. Tentacle 3. Algae 4. Coral

105 Coral polyps have a special relationship with tiny life-forms called zooxanthellae (say zoo-zan-thell-ee). These are plantlike algae that live inside a polyp's body, providing it with some of the food it needs to grow. In return, the polyps provide the algae with a safe place to live. Zooxanthellae need sunlight to survive, so they live inside a polyp's tentacles, where light can reach them.

◄ Cup corals are a non reef-building species that use their tentacles to catch prey. Coral polyps are in the same animal family as jellyfish and sea anemones, and are known as "cnidarians" (say nid-air-ee-ans).

106 Sea animals do not always go looking for food. Coral polyps cannot move around, so they grab whatever food comes their way, using their tentacles. When a tentacle touches something edible, a tiny stinger springs out and pierces the prey's skin. The tentacles draw the prey into the polyp's mouth.

CORAL REEF

▶ Coral polyps have simple bodies. Inside, there is a large stomach, or gut. A tough rocklike skeleton grows outside.

Zooxanthellae

Cnidocytes (stinging cells)

Mouth

Tentacles

Stomach

Calcium carbonate (stony skeleton)

107 **Soft-bodied corals protect themselves by growing hard cases.** These cases are made from calcium carbonate, a tough substance that turns into stone over time. Each case is cup-shaped, and the polyp grows inside it. As new polyps develop, they build on top of one another—this is how the reef grows.

108 **Adult polyps are stuck in stony cups, but young polyps can swim.** A young polyp is called a planula and it is covered in tiny hairs that help it move through the water. It may float around for days or weeks until it finds a hard surface to attach itself to, and grow into an adult.

▼ Polyps can reproduce in two ways. An egg can grow into a planula, or an adult can make a bud, which grows into a twin of itself.

4. Coral colony begins to grow through "budding."

1. Planula searches for a place to settle.

2. Planula attaches to a hard surface.

3. Polyp begins to grow a stony cup.

49

Hard and soft

109 There are two main types of coral—hard coral and soft coral. Hard coral polyps are reef builders—they use calcium carbonate to build strong structures around themselves. Soft corals are bendy, and often live alongside their stony cousins.

110 Warm water reefs can look like colorful gardens. Corals grow in many unusual shapes, appearing like bushes, trees, and mushrooms. The shape of coral depends upon the type of polyp that lives within it, and its position on the reef.

111 Some corals are easy to identify because they look just like their name. Brain corals, for example, look like brains. They grow very slowly and can reach the size of a boulder. Staghorn coral is one of the fastest-growing types, and it is an important reef builder, especially in shallow waters. Each staghorn polyp can live for around ten years, and will not reproduce until it reaches at least three years old.

▼ Corals are different shapes and sizes. The way each coral grows depends on the type of polyps that live inside the rocky structures.

Elkhorn coral

Staghorn coral

CORAL REEF

Brain coral

Mushroom coral

Lettuce coral

Sea fan

Sea whip

Soft tree coral

112 **Not all coral polyps live together in colonies.** Some types live alone in the Southern Ocean, near the Antarctic, where temperatures rarely creep above a chilly 43°F. Little is known about solitary corals, but it is thought they are sensitive to water temperature.

Where in the world?

113 Warm water coral reefs may be packed with life, but they only cover around 109,650 square miles of the Earth's surface. If you put them all together, they would still only take up the same room as a small country, such as New Zealand.

115 Coral polyps are choosy about where they grow. This is because the zooxanthellae that live with them need warmth and light to turn the Sun's energy into food. They are most likely to grow in seas and oceans within a region called the tropics, which is between the Tropic of Cancer and the Tropic of Capricorn.

◀ Damselfish and sea anemones are just two of the many animals that live on the Indian Ocean reefs.

▲ Blue-spotted stingrays hunt their prey among the Red Sea corals.

114 The Coral Triangle is an enormous region that stretches across the seas around Indonesia, Malaysia, and Papua New Guinea. It contains some of the world's most precious reefs, and is home to 3,000 species of fish and 20 species of mammals, including dugongs, whales, and dolphins.

◀ A pink porcelain crab rests on a hard coral near Malaysia, in the Coral Triangle.

CORAL REEF

116 **Dirty water is no good to coral polyps.** They prefer clear water, without the tiny particles of dirt, mud, or sand that prevent light from reaching the seabed. Reefs don't grow near river mouths, or in areas where dirt is washed from the land into the sea. Polyps are even fussy about the amount of salt dissolved in the ocean water around them.

QUIZ

Which of these are oceans, and which are seas?

Atlantic   Mediterranean
Caribbean Indian
Pacific   Coral

Answers:
Atlantic, Pacific, and Indian are oceans. Caribbean, Mediterranean, and Coral are seas.

◀ Pygmy seahorses live in the warm coral waters of the western Pacific Ocean.

◀ The Hawaiian reef fish Humuhumunukunukuapua'a is a type of triggerfish, and makes piglike snorting sounds if threatened.

Hawaiian reefs

ATLANTIC OCEAN

PACIFIC OCEAN

CARIBBEAN SEA

Mesoamerican Reef

117 **Sunlight cannot pass through water as easily as it can pass through air.** As zooxanthellae need light, their coral polyps only grow in water with a maximum depth of around 36 feet—although this varies depending on how clean the water is. This explains why warm water coral reefs grow near the land, where the water is shallow.

▲ The Caribbean reef octopus feeds at night, and eats fish and shelled animals.

CORAL SEA

◀ Giant clams live in coral reefs around the South Pacific and Indian Oceans.

SOUTHERN OCEAN

53

Types of reef

118 There are three main types of coral reef. Fringing reefs are the most common. They grow on the edges of land that are underwater, often with little or no gap in between the reef and dry land. Barrier reefs also grow where land meets the ocean, but they are separated from the land by a stretch of water, called a lagoon. Atolls are circular reefs with a lagoon in the center.

① When coral grows around an island's coasts, a fringing reef develops.

119 For a long time, no one knew how atoll reefs formed. The scientist Charles Darwin (1809–1882) suggested that most atolls had grown on the edges of islands or volcanoes that had since disappeared. He thought the islands might have sunk into the sea, but the reefs kept growing. In 1953, Darwin's theory was proved right.

② The island drops, or the sea rises, and the coral becomes a barrier reef.

CORAL REEF

120 Patch reefs form in shallow water and their tops are only visible at low tide. They are usually round or oval in shape and their outer edges are ringed by coral sand leading to beds of sea grass.

121 Bank reefs often grow in lines, or in semicircles. They have large buttress zones (the area of a reef that faces the sea) with ridges of tough coral that grow out into it. Elkhorn coral grows here because it is able to withstand strong waves.

122 The Maldives are coral islands in the Indian Ocean. As they are built from coral, most land is no more than 5 feet above sea level. People have been living in the Maldives for more than 2,000 years. There is little soil on the islands so few plants, other than coconut palms, grow well. Local people have survived by fishing and, more recently from tourism.

③ When there is no longer any sign of the island the reef is called an atoll.

Reef   Lagoon

Zones of the reef

123 **Coral reefs can grow so large that it is possible to see them from outer space.** Yet it is only the outer parts of a reef that are alive. The parts beneath the surface are dead, made up from the billions of stony cups that once housed living coral polyps.

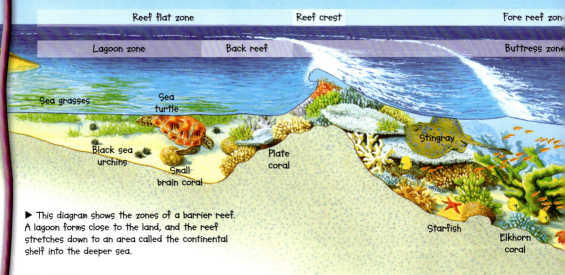

▶ This diagram shows the zones of a barrier reef. A lagoon forms close to the land, and the reef stretches down to an area called the continental shelf into the deeper sea.

124 **The part of a reef that is closest to land is called a reef flat.** It is difficult for polyps to grow well here because of the effect of the tides, which may leave the coral exposed to air for too long, and because the water can become too salty. The reef flat is home to many types of animals that scuttle around between sea grasses, dig into the soft mud, or stick to the old, dead stony structures.

125 **Most corals grow on the sides of the reef that face the sea and wind.** This area is known as the fore reef and it is warmed by ocean currents. The corals here grow upward and outward, building up layers over thousands of years. Below the fore reef is a collection of old coral material that has broken off and fallen to the seafloor. The highest part of the fore reef is the crest—the polyps that live here must be able to survive strong waves and winds.

CORAL REEF

126 **The fore reef is divided into three parts.** At the bottom, plate-shaped corals grow where there is less light. As they grow they spread out to reach the sunlight. Nearby, fan corals are stretched in front of the water currents that flow toward them. In the middle part larger, mound-shaped corals grow and near the crest, long-fingered strong corals, such as staghorn, appear.

127 **Further out to sea, a reef develops a buttress zone.** Here, large spurs or clumps of coral grow, breaking up the waves and absorbing some of their impact before they hit the rest of the reef. This is the area where sharks and barracudas are most likely to swim. Beyond the buttress zone lies the reef wall, which forms in a deeper part of the sea.

128 **Coral reefs are very slow growers.** A reef can grow about 4 inches a year if the conditions are just right. How much have you grown in the last year?

Deep reef zone

Bottlenose dolphins

Sea goldies
Sea whip
Sea fan
Maze coral
Tube-sponge
Butterfly fish
Dead coral bedrock
Lettuce coral
Star coral
Wobbegong shark
Barracudas
Whitetip reef shark

Cold water corals

129 **In the cold, dark ocean waters, coral reefs lay hidden for thousands of years.** A few of these deep sea reefs were found about 250 years ago, but it has recently been discovered that in fact, there are more cold water reefs than warm water ones.

▼ A cold water reef grows in the chilly waters of a Norwegian fjord. Visible are a basket star (1), lophelia coral (2), and a sea sponge (3).

BIG BUILDERS
Find out about some other animal architects. Use the Internet or the library to discover how bees, termites, and sociable weaver birds work together to build structures.

130 **Cold water corals live in waters between 650 and 5,000 feet deep.** The largest cold water coral reef is more than 25 miles long and up to 1.8 miles wide. Just like warm water corals, these deep sea reefs are home to a large range of animals, many of which live nowhere else on Earth.

131 Deep sea coral polyps don't have zooxanthellae, so they don't need sunlight to survive. They have to get all their food by feeding on tiny animals, called zooplankton, that drift past them. They catch these creatures with their tentacles and poison stingers, and draw them into their mouths.

◀ Zooplankton are tiny, shrimplike animals eaten by cold water corals brought to them on strong water currents.

132 Cold water corals take thousands of years to grow, but they are being destroyed at an alarming rate. Scientists believe most of the damage is caused by trawling, a type of fishing. A heavy net is pulled over, or near, the sea floor by a boat. As it is dragged along, the net catches fish, but it also damages coral and churns up mud and pollution.

133 The white coral *Lophelia pertusa* is a stony cold water coral responsible for most of the reefs in the Atlantic Ocean. Scientists have discovered more than 1,300 species of animal living on one group of reefs in the cold North Atlantic Ocean. The reefs are home to many animals, including sharks, crabs, sponges, conger eels, snails, and worms.

▼ Wolffish have powerful jaws, which they use to eat crabs and shelled animals that live around cold water corals.

The Great Barrier Reef

134 The Great Barrier Reef, on the northeast coast of Australia, is possibly the largest structure ever built by animals. It covers an area of the Coral Sea that extends for more than 12,000 miles and it took around 18 million years for the reef to grow to this enormous size.

135 It may look like one giant structure, but the Great Barrier Reef is really made up of around 3,000 smaller reefs and 1,000 islands. Although coral has grown in this region for millions of years the barrier reef only formed at the end of the last Ice Age, around 10,000 years ago.

◀ When leafy seadragons hide among seaweed they become almost invisible.

136 The Great Barrier Reef was not studied by scientists until the 18th century. British explorer James Cook (1728–1779) sailed his ship, HMS *Endeavour*, onto the reef in June 1770, and his crew had to spend six weeks repairing the damage to their craft. Ever since, explorers and scientists have been studying the structure of the reef and its wildlife.

▼ Dugongs are air-breathing animals that swim around the reef, grazing on sea grasses.

CORAL REEF

137 In 1975, the Great Barrier Reef Marine Park was set up to protect the reef. The area is home to an enormous variety of living things—there are 5,000 species of mollusks, 1,500 species of fish, 400 species of coral, 200 species of birds, 125 species of sharks, rays, and skates, 30 species of whales, dolphins, and porpoises, 14 species of sea snakes and six species of marine turtles!

▶ Groups, or shoals, of sweetlips swim around the Great Barrier Reef.

138 Native people and nearby islanders from the Torres Strait have fished in the Coral Sea for more than 60,000 years. They are known as the Traditional Owners of the Great Barrier Reef. The areas of the reef that they used in the practice of their ancient lifestyles are called the sea country. Traditional Owners work to preserve their ancient connection to the Great Barrier Reef.

◀ Like many sea snakes, olive sea snakes have a poisonous bite.

QUIZ

Can you add up all the numbers of species listed in fact 137, from mollusks to turtles? Check your answer with a calculator.

Answer:
5,000 + 1,500 + 400 + 200 + 125 + 30 + 14 + 6 = 7,275

Caribbean coral

139 **The world's second largest coral reef protects people from the effects of hurricanes (violent storms).** It is called the Mesoamerican Reef, and it lies in the Caribbean Sea, west of the Atlantic Ocean.

140 **Large areas of mangrove forest grow at the land's edge, behind the reef.** Together, the mangroves and the corals create a barrier that slows down the hurricane-force storms that often batter the Caribbean coastlines. Mangrove roots help to bind the fragile shoreline, and stop rain and river water from washing too much dirt toward the coral. They also act as nurseries for young reef fish.

▶ Bottlenose dolphins visit the reefs but they also swim out into the open ocean.

▼ There are more than 500 species of fish in the Caribbean reefs, including the pretty queen angelfish.

141 **The Mesoamerican reef is 225 million years old, 700 miles long, and home to more than 65 types of stony coral.** There are also 350 species of mollusk, and 500 types of fish, including whale sharks. These gentle giants, which are the largest fish in the world, cruise the crystal-clear waters looking for tiny animals to scoop into their enormous mouths.

CORAL REEF

▲ It is thought that whale sharks can live to be 100 years old or more. They eat small fish and krill around reefs and in deep water.

X MARKS THE SPOT!
Create a treasure map for a coral island. Fold up some paper to create creases. Tear the edges of the paper to make it look old. Remember to mark the treasure's location with a big X.

142 Throughout history, people who live near the reef have depended on its fish for food. Many of the people who live in coastal areas in countries such as Belize, Mexico, Honduras, and Guatemala have long family traditions of fishing around the reef. They discovered that swarms of fish come together during full moons to mate, and this was the perfect time to catch them in nets.

▲ Tourists enjoy the wildlife spectacle around a reef. They can snorkel, or take a ride in a glass-bottomed boat.

143 Pirates used to hide their ships among the many Caribbean islands that are dotted along the reef. Explorers came too, looking for treasure such as gold and silver, and to set up trading routes. Today, tourists flock to the area to enjoy exploring this ecosystem and its beautiful coral gardens.

Islands of fire

144 The coral reefs of Hawaii are unlike any others found on Earth. They have formed around a string of islands, called an archipelago, that developed when volcanoes erupted in the middle of the Pacific Ocean. Hawaii is about 2,000 miles from any large land mass, which means these are the world's most isolated group of islands.

145 Around one-quarter of the animals and plants that live on Hawaiian coral reefs are found nowhere else. Algae, which are seaweeds, thrive in this area—especially the stony seaweeds that help to bind reefs together and make them stronger. Algae are important because they take carbon dioxide from the air and expel oxygen, the gas that animals such as polyps need to breathe.

▼ Enormous humpback whales use the waters around Hawaii as nurseries. They stay here with their young until it is time to swim north.

146 Huge humpback whales feed on tiny krill, which are shrimplike creatures. They don't feed in the winter, so at this time of year the krill are safe.

▲▶ Hawaiian corals (1) have grown on old lava that has cooled and turned to stone (2).

147 **Volcanoes began to erupt in this area around 70 million years ago, and they are still active today.** As lava cooled and turned to stone, corals began to grow on their edges. The first polyps must have arrived as free-swimming planulas, probably from other Pacific coral reefs.

148 **Around 10,000 endangered humpback whales visit Hawaii every year.** They arrive at the warm tropical waters in the winter, after swimming all the way from their feeding grounds in Alaska. While in Hawaii, the whales give birth to their young, and care for them. They can be seen swimming, playing, and even battling with one another around the coral reefs.

◀ Green turtles lay their eggs on Hawaiian beaches because the reefs protect them from storms and waves.

149 **The islanders of Hawaii set up a marine park in 1967, to protect the reef ecosystem.** In 1956 an enormous channel, more than 200 feet wide, was blasted into the coral using dynamite to make way for a new telephone cable. The coral is now protected by law.

◀ A bobtail squid can produce light in its belly, which helps it hunt at night. The light is produced by bacteria that live on the squid.

65

A carnival of color

150 Some animals stay on the seafloor, or hide in cracks in the coral reef, but others dart, dive, and dazzle their way through the clear waters. Coral reef animals often use the colors of their shells or skins to help them lurk unseen in the shadows, or to warn other animals to stay away. When an animal uses color to hide, it is said to be camouflaged.

151 Coral fish come in beautiful patterns and brilliant colors. Good looks are important for their survival—red colors appear dark in water, stripes provide camouflage, and spots can confuse predators. Blue and yellow fish look bright to us, but they are hidden on the reef. The way sunlight is reflected off coral reefs affects the appearance of blues and yellows, making them blend in with the background.

▲▼ Coral fish come in many different colors and patterns such as the coral trout (top), regal angelfish (middle), and blue tang fish (below).

152 Squid and cuttlefish create flashes of color. These soft-bodied mollusks can change their colors in an instant to hide or attract prey toward them. They can produce skin colors of red, yellow, orange, brown, and black—and can even create patterns, such as zebra stripes, on their skin.

CORAL REEF

◀ Sea slugs are brightly colored to warn predators that they are very poisonous.

153 Land slugs are slimy and often dull in color, but coral reef slugs are bizarre, beautiful animals. Sea slugs, also called nudibranchs, don't have shells, but they do have soft, feathery gills on their backs, which help them to breathe in water. Some nudibranchs are small, but the largest ones can grow to one foot long.

154 The stripes, spines, and bright colors of a lionfish spell danger to other coral creatures. These ocean fish hunt other fish, shrimp and sea anemones. When they are threatened they react with lightning speed. Lionfish have spines on their bodies that carry deadly venom, which they raise and plunge into a predator's flesh.

▼ Lionfish hide among rocks in the daytime, and only come out at night to hunt for food. They have been known to threaten divers.

GO FISH!
Choose your favorite colorful coral fish from this book and copy it onto a large piece of paper. Use different materials, such as paints, tissue paper, buttons, and foil to show the colors and patterns.

On the attack

155 **Animals need energy to survive, and they get that energy from food.** Some reef animals graze on seaweeds and corals, but others hunt and kill to feed. Hunting animals are called predators, and their victims are called prey.

▶ When sharks, such as these lemon sharks, sense blood or food they move with speed to attack their prey.

156 **Some coral sharks aren't aggressive and divers can feed them by hand.** Bull sharks are not so relaxed around humans. They have been known to attack divers and swimmers around reefs. Sharks are drawn to coral reefs because of the thousands of fish on the reef but finding prey is not always easy when there are so many good hiding places.

157 **Cone shells look harmless, but their appearance is deceptive.** These sea snails crawl around reefs looking for prey such as worms, mollusks, and fish. They fire venom-filled darts to paralyze their prey. The dart remains attached to the cone shell, so it can draw its victim back to its body and devour it.

◀ This small animal cannot protect itself from an attack by a deadly cone shell.

158 Sea anemones and jellyfish have stingers to attack their prey, just like their coral cousins. Soft-bodied sea anemones are usually quite small and they stay attached to the sea floor, or coral, and wait for water currents to bring food their way. Jellyfish have tentacles that can stretch for many feet, hanging below their bodies. Jellyfish can swim, or they are carried along by the sea's currents.

159 Mantis shrimps are mighty crustaceans. They punch or spear their prey, using such incredible force and speed that they are regarded as one of the most powerful animals in the world for their size. These small animals are common in Australian coral reefs and parts of the Indo-Pacific reef system.

▼ A blue-ringed octopus is only 8 inches long but its saliva contains poison that is strong enough to kill a human.

▲ Box jellyfish have such deadly stings that beaches are often closed in Australia when they are present in the water.

160 Mantis shrimps are powerful punchers. They surprise their prey by hitting out at speeds of 790 feet per second.

Living together

161 **The animals and plants that live on coral reefs need each other to survive.** The close relationship between some animals is known as "symbiosis." Sometimes these partnerships give benefits to both animals, but at other times one animal gains little.

162 **Coral polyps and their zooxanthellae are best buddies.** Each zooxanthellae is made of just one cell. Like green plants, zooxanthellae make food using sunlight, water, and carbon dioxide—a gas that is in the air. This process is called photosynthesis. The food they make is eaten by the polyps. Because they need sunlight to grow, zooxanthellae live inside a polyp's tentacles where light can reach them.

▼ Clownfish can hide among the stinging tentacles of a sea anemone without getting stung.

▲ Remora fish use other animals—such as this green turtle—to hitch a ride and find food.

I DON'T BELIEVE IT!
Boxer crabs use stinging sea anemones like boxing gloves. They wave them at any predators who get too close!

163 Coral fish dance to tell other reef animals that they are ready to get cleaning. Bluestreak cleaner wrasses feed on irritating parasites that attach themselves to other fishes' bodies, causing them harm. When they are hungry the wrasses dance to attract attention, and the bigger fish line up to wait for their cleaning services.

▲ A moray eel patiently waits while a wrasse cleans its mouth.

164 Remoras are fish that hitch a ride on sharks, using specially adapted fins that work like sticky suckers. They get carried around the reef without having to spend any energy on swimming, but they may affect sharks' hunting ability by slowing them down. Remoras also latch on to dolphins and turtles.

165 Giant clams also have best buddies that they rely on to survive. These mollusks can grow up to 5 feet long and can live for more than 70 years. Zooxanthellae live on the fringes of these animals' enormous shells and provide the clams with nutrients. The clams and the algae need each other to survive, just like coral polyps and their algae.

▼ Hermit crabs depend on other shelled animals for their homes. They find empty shells and move in.

Night on the reef

166 As the Sun sets over the ocean, coral reefs change. Polyps emerge from their cups and unfurl their tentacles, producing a range of colors and movements. Creatures that were active in daylight rest in dark crevices, while others emerge to feed in the dark.

167 Coral animals that come out at night are described as nocturnal. They often have senses that help them to detect movement, light, sound, and chemicals in the inky-blue seas. Octopuses have superb night vision and long tentacles that they use to probe cracks in the reef, searching for food.

◄ Corals are nocturnal and are most active at night.

168 Coral reef spiny lobsters march through the night. At the end of the summer 100,000 of them set off on a long journey. Walking in single file toward deeper, darker water, they can travel up to 30 miles every night to reach their breeding grounds.

▼ A Christmas tree worm buries its body deep inside a coral. Only its two feeding tentacles, which look like trees, are visible.

CORAL REEF

▲ Red soldierfish have unusually large eyes, which help them to see in the dark.

169 **Fireworms are rarely seen in the day.** They live under rocks and have venom-filled spines on their backs, giving them a furry appearance. During the summer adult worms emerge once at night, during a full moon, to mate. The females produce a green glow that attracts the males in the dark water.

170 **Divers can swim with giant stingrays at night.** These enormous fish can measure up to 6.5 feet across and they often glide through the water in groups, gently flapping their "wings" to move silently and swiftly. Stingrays do not need light to hunt because they are able to detect the electricity inside other animals' bodies, and use this information to find prey such as clams and oysters.

Light organ

▲ Most flashlight fish live in deep waters, where their ability to make light is most useful. Some types, however, swim into coral waters at night.

Relying on reefs

▲ The people from this fishing village in Borneo depend on the reef for food.

171 Millions of people rely on coral reefs for their survival. These ecosystems not only support fish and other animals, they also protect coastal regions from damage by storms and wave action.

172 There are around 500 types of seaweeds living on the Great Barrier Reef alone. Seaweeds contain substances that are useful to humans. Agar comes from red seaweeds and is used to make desserts, or to thicken soups and ice cream. Alginates come from brown seaweeds and they are used to make cosmetics, thicken drinks, and in the manufacture of paper and textiles.

173 Ecosystems that have a large range of living things are often used in medical science. Many species of animals and plants that live on reefs are being used in the search for new medicines that will cure illnesses. Substances in coral polyps are being used to develop treatments for some diseases, and to help rebuild broken bones.

174 People who live around reefs have traded in coral products for thousands of years. The harvesting of red and pink corals for jewelry has caused many people to worry that the coral may be driven to extinction. Jewelry makers are asked to only use a small amount of coral every year and to only take coral from places where it will be protected as it regrows.

▶ Collecting food, such as fish, and precious coral is a traditional way to survive in many places where reefs grow.

CORAL REEF

175 Coral reefs help to support local communities through tourism. Millions of people flock to the world's reefs to enjoy nature's underwater spectacle. The money they spend there helps support local people, who provide accommodation, food, and equipment. Reefs are worth much more alive than dead. While one shark could be killed and sold for food, it is worth at least one hundred times more alive as an attraction to reef tourists.

▼ A trained guide shows tourists the delights of the Great Barrier Reef. "Ecotourism" allows visitors to enjoy the reef without damaging it.

QUIZ

What am I?
1. I am used to thicken ice cream and soups.
2. I travel and visit places of interest.
3. I grow on the reef and am often made into jewelry.

Answers:
1. Agar 2. Tourist 3. Red and pink coral

Underwater explorers

176 **Exploring a reef is a magical experience.** Bathed in warm, blue water, a diver can swim among thousands of fish that dart around the coral. As schools of small, silvery fish flash past, smaller groups of predator fish follow—fast and alert in the chase.

CREATE A CORAL
Use quick-dry clay to create your own corals, copying the pictures in this book to get the right shapes. Once dry, paint the corals in bright colors. You can also make fish or other wildlife, to build your own coral reef ecosystem.

177 **People have been fascinated by coral reefs for thousands of years.** They have enjoyed watching reef wildlife, but they have also explored in search of food and building materials. Since coral reefs grow in shallow, clear water, swimmers can enjoy them without any special equipment. Snorkels allow swimmers to breathe while their faces are in water.

178 **The best way to explore a coral reef is to go underwater.** Scuba equipment allows a diver to swim and breathe below the water's surface. Using an oxygen tank, flippers, and a face mask a diver can move carefully around a reef, watching the creatures or carrying out scientific studies.

▼ Special equipment allows divers to photograph underwater wildlife such as this Goliath grouper.

CORAL REEF

179 **Scientists have been examining coral reefs for more than 300 years.** There are many research centers and universities near large coral reefs, so scientists can collect information and learn about the reefs over many years. There are even underwater research laboratories, where scientists can study reefs close up for days at a time.

▼ Divers explore old reefs, but they also visit places where new reefs are forming on shipwrecks, to understand how they develop.

180 **Exploring reefs is fascinating, but it can be dangerous too.** Curious blacktip reef sharks may give a diver a warning nip, but a sting from a box jellyfish can be deadly. There are also poisonous sea snakes, octopuses, shellfish, and fish.

Natural coral killers

181 Some fish not only live on a reef, they eat it too. There are more than 130 types of fish, known as corallivores, that feed on corals. They eat the slimy mucus made by polyps, the polyps themselves, and even their stony cups. They like eating polyps during their breeding season because they are full of juicy, tasty eggs.

▲ Most coral-eating fish are butterfly fish. They have small mouths that can nibble at polyps and their eggs.

182 Reef-killing creatures have different eating habits around the world. In some regions, the coral-eating fish remove so much of the reef that it does not appear to grow at all. Threadfin butterfly fish in the Indian Ocean munch through large amounts of coral, but those that live around the Great Barrier Reef never eat coral. Corallivores that live in Caribbean reefs can survive on other food, too.

▼ Parrotfish change their appearance throughout their lives—they change color as they grow up!

183 Parrotfish are dazzling in their appearance, but deadly in their lifestyle. They dig at coral with their tough mouths, which are like beaks, and grind it up in their throats. This releases the zooxanthellae that are an important part of their diet. The stony parts of the coral pass through their bodies, coming out the other end as beautiful white sand.

CORAL REEF

▲ Crown-of-thorns starfish graze on corals, especially in places where the starfish's natural enemy, the trumpet shellfish, has disappeared.

184 The crown-of-thorns starfish is one of the world's most famous coral killers. It is covered in spines and can have as many as 21 "arms." This starfish eats coral by turning its mouth inside out and pouring strong juices over the polyps to dissolve their flesh. It prefers fast-growing corals over the slower-growing types. The starfish eat the polyps, but leave the stony structure behind.

185 In the 1980s, Caribbean black sea urchins, called diademas, were wiped out by a deadly disease. These sea urchins kept the reefs healthy by grazing on seaweeds. Once they had died, seaweeds took over the coral, using up space and blocking out light. Seaweed-eating fish were also struggling to survive because too many of them had been caught by fishermen. There was nothing left to control the growth of seaweed and so the coral ecosystem was changed, and may never return to its previous, healthy state.

186 Sponges are boring animals— they bore right into coral reefs! These simple animals dig right into the middle of a reef, making it weaker and more likely to collapse in storms.

Reefs at risk

187 Coral reefs are fragile ecosystems that are under threat from humans. When they are stressed, coral polyps lose their zooxanthellae, and die. Once the polyps have died the coral structure that is left appears white, and is described as "bleached."

▼ If zooxanthellae leave the coral, the polyps die. Over time, other types of algae and bacteria grow over the bleached coral.

① Healthy coral with zooxanthellae living in coral tissue.

② Zooxanthellae leave coral due to increased water temperatures.

③ Algae cover the damaged coral.

▶ Global warming, a rise in worldwide temperatures, is caused by the polluting effects of carbon dioxide. It is raising sea temperatures and is causing coral bleaching.

CORAL REEF

188 **Pollution, such as human waste (sewage) and chemicals used in farming, kills coral.** In some places, pipes carry sewage to the sea where it mixes with the seawater. Sewage contains substances that feed seaweeds but bleach corals. On land, chemicals are used on crops to help them grow or to kill pests, but they get carried out to sea by rainwater and rivers, where they damage the reef and its inhabitants.

189 **Tourists enjoy reefs, but they also put them at risk.** Visitors put pressure on local ecosystems because they need food, transport, and places to stay—which means pollution, fishing, and building. Some tourists damage reefs by standing on them or touching them, and by buying wildlife souvenirs such as coral jewelry.

190 **Damage to nearby land causes reefs to die.** When coastal areas are changed by building or digging, soil is loosened and makes its way into the sea. Soil and dirt in seawater make it cloudy and stop sunlight from reaching the zooxanthellae. The result is more coral bleaching.

▶ Coral is broken up and taken from the sea to be used as a building material.

191 **Catching and killing fish adds to the bleaching of coral reefs.** In some parts of the world, fishermen use destructive methods of fishing. They drop bombs in the water, which explode and kill whole schools of fish, turning coral to crumbs. They also use chemicals, such as cyanide, to kill or stun fish.

SAVE OUR REEFS!
Make a poster to show the different ways coral reefs are being damaged and destroyed. Include a list of top tips for tourists to help them enjoy reefs safely without harming these ecosystems.

Conserving coral

192 **Saving our coral reefs is incredibly important.** We need to protect them, or it is likely they will become the first major ecosystem to become extinct in modern times. Setting up national parks, and stopping all forms of fishing means that reefs can develop naturally.

193 **Artificial reefs have been built to replace the natural ones that are under threat.** Some man-made reefs have been successful but scientists now agree that saving the coral reefs we have is the best option. They are working to find new ways to save coral polyps and help them recover once their natural environment has been damaged.

194 **All parts of a coral reef ecosystem need to be protected.** Removing one part, such as a single type of fish, can have terrible effects on other animals and plants that live there. Supporting local people as they find alternative ways to make money and find food, rather than relying on reefs is an important step forward.

▼ To make an artificial reef, structures are placed on the seabed. Corals and other marine creatures settle here and start to create a new reef ecosystem.

CORAL REEF

195 The Komodo National Park in Indonesia covers 700 square miles of land and sea. Tourists pay to support the workers and scientists who protect their natural environment, prevent illegal fishing, and study the coral ecosystems in the park.

▲ Satellite photos of protected reefs, such as Hawaii's Pearl and Hermes atoll, help scientists find out how reefs are changing.

196 Scientists believe many coral reefs can be saved if they are protected now. Pollution is one of the biggest coral killers, and removing it could have an immediate effect on reefs' survival. This will give us more time to tackle the big problem of global warming, which will take many years.

▶ The beautiful ocean waters surrounding Komodo cover more than two-thirds of the National Park.

QUIZ

1. What do scientists believe could help save coral reefs?
2. Which word beginning with "a" means man-made?
3. Why are national parks set up?

Answers:
1. Stopping pollution 2. Artificial 3. To protect endangered ecosystems

SEASHORE

197 Seashores can be found all over the world, from icy coastlines near the Poles to sandy beaches in hot, tropical areas. As well as making unique habitats (natural homes) for many plants and animals, seashores are also very important to people. Today, large areas of Earth's 435,000-plus miles of seashores are in danger and in need of our protection.

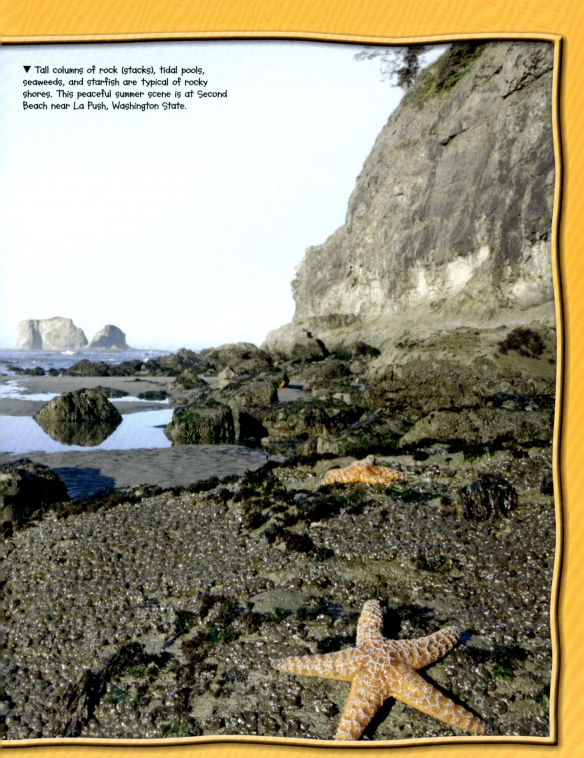

▼ Tall columns of rock (stacks), tidal pools, seaweeds, and starfish are typical of rocky shores. This peaceful summer scene is at Second Beach near La Push, Washington State.

Land meets sea

198 Seashores are places where the salty water of seas and oceans meets land made of rocks, mud, sand, or other material. A seashore is the edge of the land and the edge of the sea.

Wave-shaped icebergs, Iceland

Tourist center, Mexico

199 There are names for different kinds of seashores. If the rocks are tall and upright, they are known as cliffs. If the sand is smooth and slopes gently, it is a beach. Seashores are known as oceanic coasts, or marine or sea coastlines.

Sandy shallows, Caribbean

200 Water moves easily with waves, tides, and currents, so seashores are never still. They are complicated habitats for nature, as only certain kinds of animals and plants can live there. Wildlife must be able to survive in the changing conditions that are typical of most seashores.

Breaking glaciers, Antarctica

SEASHORE

Seafront houses, Denmark

QUIZ

1. What is a seashore?
2. Why are seashores complicated habitats for nature?
3. How many miles of seashore are there around the world?

Answers:
1. The edge of the land and the edge of the sea. 2. Because only certain kinds of animals and plants can live there 3. More than 435,000

EUROPE

ASIA

PACIFIC OCEAN

AFRICA

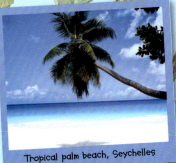

Great Barrier Reef, Australia

Tropical palm beach, Seychelles

OCEANIA

INDIAN OCEAN

201 In total, there are more than 435,000 miles of seashore. Canada is the country with the longest total seashore, at more than 125,500 miles. Indonesia is next, with 34,000 miles of seashore.

202 Some seashores are not part of the world's main network of seas and oceans. They are the seashores around the edges of large bodies of salty water that are isolated inland, such as the Caspian Sea and the Dead Sea.

ANTARCTICA

Endless battles

203 Seashores are like battlegrounds, with a continuing struggle between land and sea. The outcome depends on factors such as the land's hardness, and the strength of the winds and waves.

▶ Winds provide the energy to whip up waves that erode the shore.

Waves

Cliff

Cliff undercut by crashing waves

Rocks from fallen cliff

Sand

Pebbles

204 The sea's power is immense. Winds, waves, tides, and currents wear away (erode) the land. Big waves hit the shore with enough energy to throw around boulders the size of cars. Even small waves roll around tiny bits of rock that rub and scour the land.

205 In some places the sea wins the battle along the shore. The land is gradually rubbed away, or parts collapse and slide into the water. The pieces, or particles, are swept away by waves, tides, and currents.

▼ In East Anglia, England, soft coastal rocks are worn away by up to 16 feet each year. Houses that were once inland end up as rubble underwater.

▲ These granite rocks in Nova Scotia, Canada, have hardly changed for hundreds of years.

▲ Chalk cliffs in southern England are eaten away by waves, leaving piles of broken pieces at their bases.

206 How the seashore's land resists the eroding power of the sea depends on the types of rocks.
Hard rocks, such as granite, are tough and can resist erosion for centuries. Softer rocks, such as chalk and mudstone, erode several feet each year.

207 In other places, the land wins the battle.
New land can be formed from piles of particles, such as sand or silt, moved by the water from coasts elsewhere or from the deep sea. Particles sink and settle as layers, called sediments, that build up.

CLIFF COLLAPSE!
You will need:
large, deep tray or bowl   wet play sand   water

Make a steep cliff in the tray or bowl by piling up wetted sand on one side. Then gently pour in the water. Swish the water with your hand to make waves. Watch how they eat into the cliff and make it fall down.

208 Movements in the Earth can change seashores.
Land can bend and buckle over centuries, so coasts slowly rise. Earthquakes can lift land by several feet in a few seconds. A volcano near the coast can spill its red-hot lava into the sea, where it cools as hard, new rock.

▶ Lava meets the sea in Hawaii. Sea water makes volcanic lava cool suddenly in a cloud of steam.

89

Tides, currents, and winds

209 Almost all seashores have tides, which affect the way the land is worn away. Tides alter the amount of time that a particular patch of the shore is underwater or exposed to the air, so they also affect coastal habitats and wildlife.

210 The tidal range is the difference in height between high and low tide. In the Bay of Fundy in Canada it is 56 feet, and in parts of the Mediterranean Sea it is less than one foot.

211 Tides are caused by the pulling power or gravity of the Moon and Sun, and the daily spinning of Earth. A high tide occurs about 12.5 hours after the previous high tide, with low tides midway between.

◀ The Moon's gravity pulls the sea into "bulges" on the near and opposite sides, where it is high tide. Inbetween is low tide. As the Earth spins daily, the "bulge" travels around the planet.

212 Spring tides are extra high— the water level rises more than normal. They happen when the Moon and Sun are in line with the Earth, adding their gravities together every 14 days (two weeks). Neap tides are extra low, when the Sun and Moon are at right angles, so their pulling strengths partly cancel each other out. A neap tide occurs seven days after a spring tide.

▼ At new Moon and full Moon, the Sun, Moon, and Earth are in a straight line, causing spring tides. At the first and last quarters of the Moon, the Sun and Moon are not aligned, so neap tides occur.

④ **Splash zone** has lichens, which receive wave spray.

③ **Upper intertidal zone** is exposed to air most of the time—there are green wrack seaweeds and limpets.

② **Mid intertidal zone** is submerged half of the time—there are mussels, barnacles, hermit crabs, and brown seaweeds.

① **Lower intertidal zone** is usually underwater—there are anemones, starfish, fish, and red seaweeds.

▲ The amount of time underwater determines which animals and plants live along a rocky shore.

213 Tides produce "zones" along seashores, from the high tide zone to the low tide zone. Different seaweeds and animals are adapted to each zone.

214 Ocean currents affect the seashore. A current flowing toward the shore can bring particles of sediment to add to the land. A current flowing away sweeps sediment out to sea. Currents also alter the direction and power of waves.

215 If a wind blows waves at an angle onto a beach, each wave carries particles of sand upward and sideways. When they recede, the particles roll back. Particles gradually zigzag along the shore—a process called longshore drift. Groynes built into the sea help to control it, so beaches don't wash away.

Seashore features

216 On a typical seashore, the struggle between land and sea produces various features. Much depends on the balance between the sea's wearing away of the land, and the formation of new land by particles settling in layers, known as sedimentation.

217 Hard or tough rocks can resist the sea's eroding power. They form tall cliffs and headlands that erode slowly. Softer rocks break apart more easily. The waves erode them at sea level, which is known as undercutting. The whole shore collapses as boulders tumble into the water.

218 Waves and other shore-eroding forces may gradually cut through a headland, forming a cave. This can get worn through to form an arch of rock. When the arch collapses it leaves an isolated tall piece of rock, called a stack.

▲ In this bay, waves and currents wash sediments with increasing power from right to left. Wall-like groynes or breakwaters lessen longshore drift.

SEASHORE

Labels on illustration: Circular bay, Cave, Cliffs, Waves, River, Delta, Mudflats (bare mud near delta), Saltmarsh (with plants), Dunes, Sandy beach

QUIZ

Match these record-breaking coastal features to their countries.
1. The longest spit, 62 miles.
2. The tallest sea stack, 1,800 feet.
3. The tallest seashore cliffs, 5,120 feet.

A. Australia   B. Greenland   C. Lithuania and Russia

Answers: 1C 2A 3B

219 Waves and onshore currents flowing toward the land bring sediments to make low shores and mounds of sand, mud, and silt. These can lengthen to form long spits. During extra-high spring tides these sediments grow higher.

220 Depending on winds and currents, a huge rounded scoop may be carved along the seashore to form a bay. In sheltered parts of the bay, particles of sand gather to form a beach. As the bay gets more curved, it can break through the land behind to leave an island.

221 The area where a river flows into the sea is a type of shore known as an estuary, or river mouth. Particles of sand and mud may build up in sheltered areas, forming low mudflats and saltmarshes.

Coast to coast

222 A seashore's features and wildlife depend on its location. Seashores near the Poles are cold most of the year and the sea may freeze for months. Almost no life can survive there.

◀ Antarctic coasts are mostly floating sheets and lumps of ice. Crabeater seals rest at the ice edge after feeding in the almost freezing water.

223 Some cold seashores have no land. Glaciers and ice shelves spread outward, so the sea meets ice, not land. The edge of the ice may have smooth slopes and platforms cut by the waves. Jagged chunks of ice crack off and fall into the water as floating icebergs.

224 In tropical regions around the middle of the Earth, seashore conditions are very different. It is warm for most of the year and many forms of life flourish, including seaweeds, fish, crabs, prawns, starfish, and corals.

▼ Tropical seashores include coral reefs, like this one near Komodo Island, Southeast Asia, with huge biodiversity (range of living things).

SEASHORE

225 **Exposure to wind is a powerful factor in the shaping of a shoreline.** A windward seashore is exposed to strong prevailing winds. The winds make waves that hit the shore hard, sending salty spray to great heights. This type of shore has very different animals and plants from a leeward seashore, which is sheltered from the main winds.

226 **Yearly seasons have an effect on seashores and their wildlife.** Usually there is rough weather in winter, with winds and storms that increase land erosion. Some wildlife moves away from the shore in winter—birds fly inland while lobsters and fish move into deeper water.

227 **The slope of the seabed at the shore is very important, affecting the size and number of waves.** A seabed with a very shallow slope tends to produce smaller waves. A steep slope up to the beach gives bigger waves that erode the land faster, but are good for surfing!

LET'S SURF!

You will need:
sink or bathtub   water   tray

Put 4 inches of water into the sink or bathtub. Hold the tray at one end, at an angle so that part of it slopes into the water like a beach. Swish your other hand in the water to make waves hit the "beach." How does altering the tray's angle from low to high affect the waves?

▲ A big winter storm, such as this one in Sussex, UK, can smash even the strongest sea defenses, which have to be repaired regularly.

Saltmarshes and mudflats

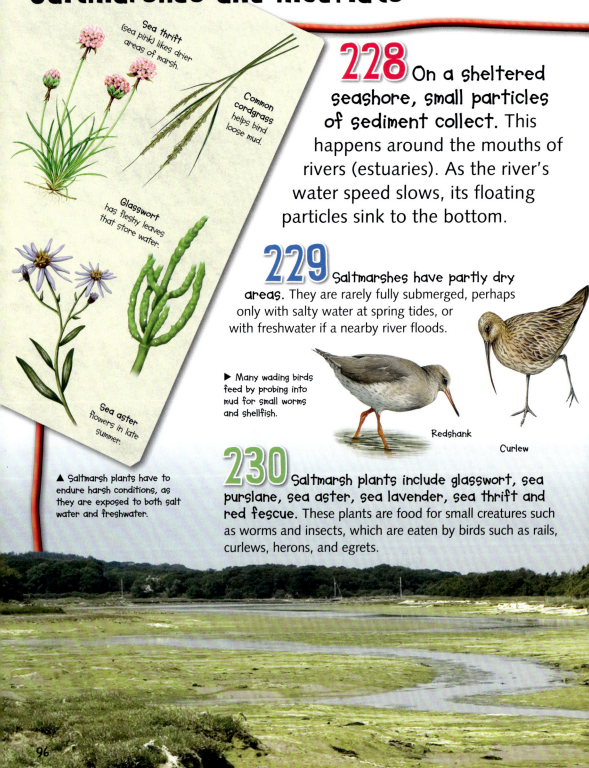

Sea thrift (sea pink) likes drier areas of marsh.

Common cordgrass helps bind loose mud.

Glasswort has fleshy leaves that store water.

Sea aster flowers in late summer.

▲ Saltmarsh plants have to endure harsh conditions, as they are exposed to both salt water and freshwater.

228 On a sheltered seashore, small particles of sediment collect. This happens around the mouths of rivers (estuaries). As the river's water speed slows, its floating particles sink to the bottom.

229 Saltmarshes have partly dry areas. They are rarely fully submerged, perhaps only with salty water at spring tides, or with freshwater if a nearby river floods.

▶ Many wading birds feed by probing into mud for small worms and shellfish.

Redshank

Curlew

230 Saltmarsh plants include glasswort, sea purslane, sea aster, sea lavender, sea thrift and red fescue. These plants are food for small creatures such as worms and insects, which are eaten by birds such as rails, curlews, herons, and egrets.

SEASHORE

231 **Mudflats are usually lower and wetter than saltmarshes, as every high tide washes over them.** Plants find it difficult to take root in these conditions, but a few, such as rice grass, cordgrass, and eel grass, manage. Cordgrass grows in the wetter regions of saltmarshes around the world. It has glands to get rid of unwanted salt taken in from sea water.

232 **Most mudflat animal life is under the surface.** There are burrowing animals such as ragworms, mud shrimps, and ghost crabs, and shelled creatures such as spire shells, tower shells, cockles, and various types of clams. Birds, especially waders such as godwits, knots, and snipes, fly in at low tide to probe for these creatures.

▼ Each year, summer plants grow into the calm waters of saltmarshes, spreading their greenery into the channels. However fall storms soon wash them away.

Soft-shell clams like muddy shores best.

Laver spire shells are also called mudsnails.

Tower shells feed in both sand and silt.

Common cockles filter sea water for food.

▲ Shelled animals with two shell halves are called bivalves. Spiral ones are types of sea snails.

233 **Mudflats teem with life.** In some mudflats, the numbers of small shellfish, called spire shells, are greater than 50,000 in just 3 square feet!

Sandy beaches

234 **Sandy shores need gentle winds, waves, and currents that are still strong enough to wash away silt and mud.** Just above high tide, any rain quickly drains away between the grains of sand, so it is too dry for land plants to grow. Below this, the grains move with wind, waves, and tides, so few sea plants can grow there either.

236 **Searching along the beach strandline is known as beachcombing.** It is especially rewarding after a big storm!

235 **Most sandy shore life is under the surface.** Animals hide under the sand while the tide is out. As it rises, it brings with it tiny plants and animals, known as plankton, and bits of dead plants and creatures. Shrimps, lugworms, clams, tellins, scallops, and heart urchins burrow through the sand or filter the water to feed.

237 **Small sandy shore animals are meals for bigger predators that follow the tide, including cuttlefish, octopus, and fish such as sea bass and flatfish.** The giant sea bass of North Pacific shores grows to more than 6 feet long and weighs 550 pounds.

▼ As the tide comes in, creatures hidden in the sand come out and start to feed—but predators are ready to eat them.

Jellyfish may get washed up onto the beach and stranded.

Cuttlefish grab prey with their tentacles.

Sand eels feed on the bottom.

Flatfish have colors similar to the seabed.

Common shrimps half hide in burrows.

SEASHORE

▼ Fencing helps to keep sand dunes still, so grasses can start to grow.

238 As high tide retreats, it leaves a ribbon of washed up debris along a beach, called the **strandline**. Animals including gulls, foxes, otters, and lizards scavenge here for food, such as dead fish and crabs.

239 On some sandy shores, onshore winds blow the sand grains up the beach toward the land. Mounds, ridges, and hills form seashore habitats called sand dunes. Marram grass can survive the wind and dryness, and its roots stop the grains blowing away, stabilizing the dunes.

Gulls scavenge in strand debris.

Otters look for fish and crabs.

Lizards grab any food bits.

Lugworm casts are squiggly piles.

Sand hole made by crab.

Toads eat sandhoppers.

Razor shells burrow very deep.

Lugworms in U-shaped burrows.

Masked crabs are safe in their burrows.

99

Mangrove swamps

240 Mangrove swamps are unusual shore habitats. They occur in the tropics where wind, waves, and currents are weak, allowing mud to collect. The mud has no tiny air pockets, which land plants need to take oxygen from.

◀ Shoreline mangroves, here in East Africa, form a thick tangle where no other plants grow. These mangrove trees have stilt roots.

241 Mangrove trees use their unusual roots to get oxygen from the air. Some have stilt or prop roots, which hold the tree above the mud and water so it can take in oxygen through tiny holes in its bark. Others have aerial roots covered with tiny holes that poke above the mud into the air.

▼ Black mangroves, like these in Florida, have aerial roots covered with tiny holes that poke above the mud into the air.

SEASHORE

242 **Mangrove swamps teem with wildlife.** The biggest creatures include dugongs and manatees (large marine mammals) that eat the fallen leaves, flowers, and fruits of mangrove trees. Fish and turtles swim among the roots, while mangrove and fiddler crabs burrow in the mud or climb the roots.

▲ Mangrove roots, stems, and seaweeds form an underwater jungle where small predators, such as this lemon shark pup, hunt for victims.

243 **Roosting birds, land crabs, mangrove snakes, and fishing cats live in mangroves.** In South and Southeast Asia, tigers slink between the trees looking for prey. One of the strangest inhabitants is the proboscis monkey. The male has a long, floppy nose, which can be up to 3 inches in length.

Male proboscis monkey

Female proboscis monkey

▶ Proboscis monkeys eat mainly mangrove leaves and fruits, and they are excellent swimmers.

Baby proboscis monkey

QUIZ

Match these mangrove creatures with their food.
1. White-bellied mangrove snake
2. Tiger 3. Proboscis monkey

A. Mangrove leaves, buds, flowers, and fruits
B. Large prey, such as monkeys and deer
C. Small crabs and fish

Answers:
1C 2B 3A

101

Shingle and pebbles

244 One of the harshest seashore habitats is the shingle, pebble, or gravel beach. Fairly strong winds, waves, and currents wash away smaller particles, such as silt and sand, leaving behind lumps of rock and stone. Sand or mud may collect over time, but a strong storm's crashing waves wash them away.

◀ On this New Zealand shingle beach, a storm has washed away some of the smaller pebbles to leave a line of larger cobbles, which protect the shingle higher up.

HIDDEN EGGS

You will need:
smooth, rounded pebbles   tray   watercolor paints and brush   three hard-boiled eggs

Lay out the pebbles on the tray and look at their colors and patterns. Paint the eggs to match the pebbles. Now, place the eggs among the pebbles. Are they so well camouflaged that your friends can't spot them?

245 Waves roll shingle and pebbles around, wearing away their sharp edges and making them smooth and rounded. Plants are in danger of being crushed by the waves, but salsify, sea kale, and sea blite gain a roothold. Lichens, combinations of fungi or molds, and simple plants known as algae, coat the stones.

SEASHORE

◀ Sea kale usually grows just above the high tide mark.

Ringlike black band around neck

Camouflaged eggs

Fleshy folded leaves

Plentiful small white flowers

246 Animals forage along the strandline, where debris is left by the receding high tide. Ringed plovers, little terns, and oystercatchers lay their eggs in a small scrape or hollow. The eggs are perfectly camouflaged because they look similar to the pebbles around them.

▲ The ringed plover checks its eggs before going off to feed on small creatures.

247 Shingle and pebble shores are very mobile. Storms and powerful currents can shift them from place to place, or even wash them into the sea. Pebbles can build up over years into a long ridge called a shingle spit. The spit shelters the sea behind it and allows other kinds of coastlines to form, such as mudflats, lagoons, or sandy beaches.

◀ The 10-miles shingle spit of Orford Ness, east England, is bare on the seaward side, but has plants on the sheltered side bordering the River Alde.

Estuaries and lagoons

▲ This maze of channels and sandbanks at the mouth of Australia's Murray River changes over months and years, especially during winter storms.

248 An estuary is the end of a river at the coast, where it flows into the sea. The river might emerge through a narrow gap. Or it can gradually widen as it approaches the sea, so that at the shore it is so wide you cannot see from one side to the other.

249 The river water slows down as it flows into the sea and loses its movement energy. As this happens, its sediment particles settle out in order of size. This is known as sediment sorting or grading. As particles settle to the bottom, they may form a spreading area in the river mouth called a delta.

250 Estuaries are halfway habitats, with freshwater toward the river and salt water toward the sea. There is an ever-changing mixture in between due to tides, currents, and rainfall. This partly salty water is known as brackish.

▶ Grizzly bears dig up tasty shellfish on an estuary beach in Canada.

SEASHORE

▶ This circular island in the Maldives, called a coral atoll, has a lagoon in the middle.

251 A lagoon is a sheltered area behind some kind of barrier, such as a ridge of shingle or a coral reef. Protected from the full force of the waves, lagoons are usually calm, warm, shallow, and full of life.

▼ Blacktip reef sharks often gather in shallow lagoons and estuaries in the breeding season to find partners and mate. They lay eggs here, where the baby sharks are safer from large predators than in the open water.

252 The tallest inhabitants in some coastal lagoons are flamingos, such as the American and greater flamingo. They filter tiny shrimps, shellfish, and plants from the water with the brushlike bristles inside their beaks.

Rocky shores and pools

253 Where the land is made from hard rock, different kinds of rocky shores form. They vary with the rock's hardness, the size of the pieces, and whether the shore is exposed to wind, waves, and currents. Tidal zones (see page 91) are usually visible on these shores with "lines" of seaweeds.

▲ Some seaweeds, such as kelps, have a suckerlike part, the holdfast, to fix them to rocks.

254 Channeled wrack, a green seaweed, often grows high on the shore with bladderwrack. Knotted rack grows slightly lower. Toward the low tide area are brown seaweeds, such as oarweeds and kelps, and even lower are red seaweeds. These plants vary depending on the coast's exposure to wind and waves.

▼ Seaweeds anchor to any stable object, such as these mostly buried rocks on a beach in France.

SEASHORE

KEY
1. Anemone
2. Mussel
3. Goby
4. Bladderwrack seaweed
5. Hermit crab
6. Topshell
7. Limpet
8. Razor shell
9. Sea urchin
10. Sponge
11. Shore crab
12. Velvet crab
13. Prawn
14. Starfish

▼ A busy rock pool is a mini habitat crawling with plants, herbivorous animals, and predators.

255 Fixed-down creatures such as barnacles and mussels live on the bare rocks of the mid-tidal zones. As the tide comes in they filter tiny edible particles from the water. Limpets hold onto the rocks firmly and move slowly, scraping off plant growth. Seaweeds form forests for smaller animals such as shellfish, crabs, prawns, and fish such as gobies and blennies, as well as starfish, anemones, sea mats, and sea squirts.

256 Seashore rock pools are left behind as the tide retreats. They are miniature communities of animals and plants. The seaweeds capture the Sun's light energy for growth. Herbivorous animals such as periwinkles and limpets eat the plants. Predators ranging from whelks to octopus hide among the crevices and prey on the herbivores.

Visitors to the shore

257 **Many animals visit seashores.** Some of them come to feed or breed. Others stop there to rest during long journeys or to escape danger such as predators or harsh conditions inland or out at sea. Otters like to catch fish and crabs in the pools and shallows.

▲ Sea lion pups may feed on their mother's milk for up to one year.

258 **Seals, sea lions, and walruses are ideally suited to diving, swimming, and feeding at sea.** But they come ashore to beaches or rocks to rest and sunbathe.

◄ Male Southern elephant seals roar and fight rivals on the beach. Winners get to mate with females.

259 **Seals and sea lions have their young (pups) along the seashore.** The pups feed on their mothers' milk, then stay ashore while the mothers return to the sea to catch food. Within two or three weeks the pups can swim and dive.

SEASHORE

▲ Terns flock down to rest overnight on a remote beach before continuing their migration.

QUIZ
Match these seashore visitors to their regions.
1. Leatherback turtle
2. Walrus
3. Adélie penguin

A. All warm and cool seas
B. Antarctic coasts
C. Arctic coasts

Answers:
1A 2C 3B

260 **Visiting birds use seashores as resting places on their long yearly journeys (migrations).** Some move to the coast for winter, when inland waters freeze. Migrants include waders or shorebirds such as dunlins, sandpipers, godwits, and curlews. Wildfowl such as ducks, geese, and swans also stop over on migration or overwinter on the shore.

▶ After laying about 150 eggs into the hole she dug, this female green turtle pushes sand on top to close the hole before returning to the water.

261 **Among the rarest shore visitors is the sea turtle.** The female hauls herself up the beach under cover of darkness, scoops a large hole with her flippers, lays her eggs in it, covers them, and lumbers back to the sea. Weeks later the baby turtles hatch and dig their way to the surface. Then it's a race to the sea—many will be eaten by gathering predators on the way.

109

Above the seashore

262 The skies above many seashores are busy with all kinds of flying animals. Several kinds of birds rest or nest along the shore, flying out to sea or inland to feed.

◀ Different kinds of birds tend to perch and nest at different heights along the cliffs.

263 Coastal cliffs are safe nesting places for many different seabirds. It is difficult for predators, such as foxes, lizards, or snakes, to reach the birds' eggs and chicks on steep rocky ledges. Cliff nesters include fulmars, puffins, Manx shearwaters, and gannets.

KEY
1. Great black-backed gull
2. Lesser black-backed gull
3. Herring gull
4. Rock dove
5. Chough
6. Puffin
7. Guillemot
8. Razorbill
9. Rock pipit
10. Fulmar
11. Kittiwake
12. Black guillemot

SEASHORE

▲ The caracara, a type of falcon, pecks the flesh from mussels.

266 As darkness falls along the shore, most birds settle to rest. The nocturnal (nighttime) fliers such as owls and bats come out. The coastal sheathtail bat of Australia and Papua New Guinea feeds mainly on beetles and other insects. Along the shores of southwest North America, the fishing bat swoops down to catch fish, crabs, and other creatures.

264 Some birds fly along coasts when looking for food, including gulls, waders, wildfowl, and birds of prey. There are several types of sea eagle, including the bald eagle (national emblem of the U.S.A.) and the even more powerful Steller's sea eagle.

267 Flying insects are also common along seashores, especially in the summer. Beetles and flies buzz around washed-up rotting seaweeds, fish, and other debris. Butterflies flutter along the upper shore and cliffs, searching for sweet nectar in the flowers. They include the bitterbush blue butterfly of Australia, and North America's rare Lange's metalmark butterfly, which inhabits sand dunes.

▶ Grayling butterflies sunbathe on sea holly and shore rocks.

Sea holly

265 The peregrine falcon hunts along the shore as well as inland. It kills other birds by power diving onto them at speeds of more than 125 miles an hour, making it the world's fastest animal.

Skins, shells, and stars

268 Many kinds of small seashore fish, such as gobies, shannies, and blennies, don't have scales. They are covered in tough, smooth, slippery skin. This helps them to wriggle through seaweed and slip away from rolling pebbles.

▲ The soft-bodied hermit crab uses an empty sea-snail shell for protection, finding a larger one as it grows.

▼ Mudskippers can stay out of water for several hours and "skip" on their front fins.

269 Crabs scuttle and swim across the shore. They have eight walking legs and two strong pincers (chelae). Many are scavengers, eating whatever they can find. Others hunt small fish and similar creatures. Their long-bodied cousins are lobsters, which grow to 3 feet long.

FISHY FACTS!

You will need:
notebook pen

Next time you're in a supermarket or fishmonger, look for the various kinds of fish and shellfish on sale—cod, salmon, prawns, mussels, and so on. Make a list of them. Do some research and find out which ones live along seashores— probably quite a few!

SEASHORE

270 Seashore anemones look like jelly blobs when the tide is out and colorful flowers when it's in. Anemones are predatory animals. Their stinging tentacles grab fish, shrimps, and other prey, paralyze them, and pass them to the mouth.

271 Starfish are slow but deadly hunters. They grab shellfish such as mussels, and gradually pull their shell halves apart. The starfish then turns its stomach inside out through its mouth, and pushes this through the gap between the shell halves to digest the flesh within.

▼ The scallop snaps its two shell valves shut, creating a jet of water that pushes it away from danger, such as a hungry starfish.

272 Shellfish abound on the seashore. Whelks and topshells have snaillike curly shells. Cowries have beautifully patterned shells in bright colors. Bivalve shellfish such as clams, oysters, cockles, and scallops have two halves (valves) to the shell.

▶ Goose barnacles are related to crabs. Their feathery feeding tentacles filter tiny bits of food from sea water.

Seashore dangers

273 Seashores can be hit by many types of natural disasters. Among the most deadly are giant waves called tsunamis. These are usually set off by underwater earthquakes, volcanoes, or landslides, which shake the sea bed and push water into massive ripples that spread out until they reach a shore.

③ Wave gets taller but slower as it approaches the coast.
② An upward wave is formed.
④ Wave crashes or breaks onto the coast.
① Undersea earthquake moves large amount of water.

▲ As tsunami waves enter shallow water, they move more slowly but grow taller.

274 In 1958, in Lituya Bay, Alaska, an earthquake caused a mega tsunami. The wave was 1,640 feet high caused by rock and ice falling into the water.

275 The high winds of hurricanes, typhoons, and tornadoes can whip up giant waves. They crash on the shore, smash buildings, flood far inland, and cause immense destruction. In 2008, typhoon Nargis hit Burma (Myanmar) in Southeast Asia. It killed more than 200,000 people, made millions homeless, and flooded vast areas with salt water, making the land useless for growing crops.

▼ Tsunamis can flood whole towns along the coast, washing salt water and mud everywhere. Houses were flattened near the coast of Banda Aceh, Indonesia, after a tsunami in 2004.

SEASHORE

▲ In the past, being a lighthouse-keeper was a vital but lonely job, with weeks alone tending the lamp and its machinery. Today most lighthouses, such as Fanad Head in northwest Ireland, are electric and mostly automatic.

276 For centuries fire beacons, lanterns, lighthouses, and lightships have warned boats and ships about dangerous shores. Hazards include running aground on a sandbank or hitting rocks just under the surface. Each lighthouse flashes at a different time interval so sailors can identify it.

Top 5 dangers to divers

1 Getting snagged or caught in old nets, cables, ropes, and fishing lines.

2 Being pushed onto sharp-edged corals, underwater girders, or boat wrecks by currents.

3 Waves stirring up the seabed, making it easy to get lost in the cloudy water.

4 Poisonous animals such as sea wasps, box jellyfish, stingrays, lionfish, and stonefish.

5 Big fierce fish such as barracudas, tiger sharks, great whites, and bull sharks.

▼ The stonefish's fin spines can jab deadly venom into the skin.

Venom canal
Sharp tip
Venom gland

▼ Fire coral is named after the burning pain it causes if touched.

277 Even just walking along a shore or paddling in shallow water can be dangerous, especially in tropical regions. There may be poisonous animals such as jellyfish, weeverfish, stonefish, and shellfish known as coneshells, all of which have stings that can kill.

People and seashores

278 People have lived along seashores and coastlines for thousands of years. Settlers could hunt and gather food from the sea. They could travel by boat along the coast, up rivers to inland areas and across the sea to other regions. These boats carried raw materials, food, and goods for trading.

279 Foods from the seashore include fish, octopus, crabs, and lobsters caught with nets, spears, or hooks and lines. Shellfish such as cockles, mussels, scallops, limpets, and winkles are gathered by hand. Seaweeds can be harvested for food or to obtain chemicals used in many processes from dyeing textiles to glassmaking.

280 Seashore plants were once used to make glass. Glassworts, samphires, and saltworts were harvested and burned to obtain the substance soda ash, or sodium carbonate, used in glassmaking.

281 Seashores are important in traditional arts, crafts, and religions. Driftwood is carved into fantastic shapes, seashells are collected for their beauty, and necklaces made of sharks' teeth supposedly give strength to the wearer. Gods and spirits from the sea feature in many religions, faiths, and customs, such as Kauhuhu the shark god of Hawaii.

▼ Sri Lankan fishermen perch on poles and watch for fish passing below as the tide changes.

▲ Lights never go out in Hong Kong (China) harbor, one of the world's busiest seaports.

▼ More than 150,000 troops landed on Normandy beaches in France on D-Day, June 6, 1944.

282 In recent times, large areas of coastal land in places such as the Netherlands, India, Bangladesh, and southern U.S.A. have been made into rich farmlands. Sea walls and other defenses keep the waves at bay. Reclaimed land is used for factories and industry, dwellings as in Venice and Singapore, and airport runways as in Sydney, Singapore, and Hong Kong (China).

▼ Holiday developments completely destroy natural coasts, with increased travel by air and sea as tourists come and go.

283 Seashores have featured in empires and battles through the ages. Seafaring and trading centers, such as Constantinople (now Istanbul), Venice, and London, were once hubs of great empires. Castles and forts keep out seaborne invaders. World War II's D-Day seaborne invasion of France's Normandy coastline in 1944 was the largest military event in history.

Seaside adventures

284 In modern times, seashores have become places for fun, leisure, and adventure. People relax, sunbathe, play games and sports, and view buildings and monuments. In many countries, more than half of all tourism business is along coasts.

▲ Scuba-divers should "take nothing but photographs and memories," leaving wildlife completely untouched.

▼ Adding just the right amount of water makes the sand firm for sculpting.

285 Fun activities at the seashore include swimming, snorkelling, scuba diving, kite flying, and building sandcastles. People also paint, draw, and photograph beautiful scenes of the waves, shore, sky, and Sun. Many seaside resorts have sand sculpture competitions, where contestants produce amazing shapes from just sand and water.

SEASHORE

286 Some seashores attract sportspeople, especially large flat beaches, which can be used by horse riders, runners, and racers. Sand racing takes many forms, from land yachts with wheels blown along by sails, to record-breaking racing cars. Softer sand is best for volleyball, football, bowls, and similar ball games.

SAND SCULPTING

You will need:
half a bucket of clean play sand
large tray   small cup   water

Start with dry sand. Pour it onto the tray and try to shape it into a tower or castle. Put it back in the bucket, mix in one cup of water and try again. Then add another cup, try again, and so on. At what stage is the sand best for shaping and sculpting?

287 In shallow water along the shore, people do sports such as surfing, windsurfing, kitesurfing, waterskiing, jetskiing, and paragliding. There is also rod fishing, spear fishing, beach netting, and other pastimes, which could result in a tasty meal.

▼ Bondi Beach near Sydney, Australia, is famous for its surfing and lifesaving displays—but it also gets very crowded.

288 Sea walls and pleasure piers extend from the shore, allowing people to stroll along, do some sea fishing, or see a show in the theater at the end. The longest pleasure pier in the world is Southend Pier in Essex, England, at 7,080 feet.

▼ Pleasure piers, such as Southend Pier, were popular in the last century, but few new ones are built.

Trade and power

▶ Modern ports, such as this one in Singapore, are busy day and night all through the year.

289 Cities, ports, and industrial centers have been set up along seashores all over the world. There are harbors, docks, wharves, and warehouses where cargo ships and passengers come and go, as part of global trade and travel.

290 Today's world uses energy at an increasing rate and many energy sources come through or from seashores. Petroleum (oil) and gas supertankers arrive at coastal storage centers, depots, and refineries, where they load or unload their cargoes.

291 Many electricity-generating power stations are along seashores. Big ships can unload supplies of coal, oil, gas, and other energy sources directly to them. Another reason is that they can use sea water to cool their generating equipment, to make electricity more efficiently.

▶ At Mossel Bay, South Africa, dozens of giant tanks store natural gas from wells out at sea.

292 The biggest cargo container ships may carry more than 14,000 standard metalbox containers. Put end to end they would stretch almost 56 miles!

293 Electricity can be generated at seashores, especially from the moving water of tides and waves. The flowing water turns underwater turbine blades connected to generators when the tide comes in and goes out. Wave power is more difficult to harness because big storms can smash the generating equipment.

294 Factories making products are often sited along the coast. Cargo ships bring raw materials, such as coal, oil, and metal ores, and take away finished products ranging from MP3 players to giant trucks. Unfortunately, factory wastes and unwanted chemicals may flow or discharge along pipes into the sea.

▲ The Limpet is one type of small wave-power generator being tested in Scotland.

121

Seashores in trouble

295 Seashores and their animals and plants face all sorts of threats and dangers. Pollution occurs in many forms, such as oil spills, chemical waste from factories, and dirty water and sewage from towns and cities. All kinds of garbage litters the shore.

▲ In Namibia, Africa, desert comes right to the sea. Many ships have run aground and been wrecked, rusting away along this "Skeleton Coast."

296 Along some busy beaches, more than one in ten particles or grains is not sand—it is plastic. Known as "beach confetti," this plastic sand is a growing problem worldwide.

297 Seashore tourist centers and resorts may be fun, but they cause big problems. They bring coastal roads, seaports and airports, bright lights, activity, and noise to the shore and shallow waters. This frightens away shore creatures such as fish, crabs, seals, sea turtles, and birds.

▼ This pile of plastic and other debris in Dorset, England, is typical of the pollution washed up after a storm.

SEASHORE

298 Modern shore fishing and food harvesting does immense damage. Powerful boats with huge nets scour and scrape up life from the water and sea bed, leaving them empty. People fish with dynamite and poisonous chemicals. Unique habitats are destroyed and will take years to recover.

▲ Plastic nets and lines do not rot away naturally. They may trap animals, such as this green turtle, for months.

299 Global warming and climate change are looming problems for the whole Earth—especially seashores. Sea levels will rise, altering the shapes of coasts, wiping out natural shore habitats and man-made ones, and flooding low-lying land beyond, from wild areas to cities and rich farmland.

300 With global warming and climate change, more extreme weather may come along coasts. Hurricanes, typhoons, and other storms could happen more often, causing destruction along the shores. Today's coastal flood defenses, such as sea walls and estuary barriers, will be overwhelmed.

▼ Recycled materials can be used as sea walls to protect against rising sea levels—but they only last a few years.

SHARKS

301 Sharks are meat-eating fish, and nearly all of them live in the sea. Many are active hunters and chase after their prey. Some lie in wait to grab their victims. Other kinds are scavengers, feasting on the dead bodies of animals such as whales and seals.

◀ Gray reef sharks are often seen in groups around coral islands, especially at night when they are most active. They are curious sharks that often swim close to divers, and near the water's surface.

Super swimmers

302 Nearly all sharks have slim, streamlined bodies. This makes them fast swimmers—they slip through the water easily and travel at speed. One of the fastest sharks is the shortfin mako. It swims at more than 34 miles an hour—much faster than a champion human sprinter can run.

▲ The mako shark is slim and speedy, and races after prey such as mackerel, tuna, and squid. It can leap more than 30 feet out of the water.

Caudal fin (tail)
Upper lobe
Second dorsal fin
First dorsal fin
Lower lobe
Anal fin
Pelvic fin
Pectoral fin

303 Sharks have several fins that help them to swim and cut through the water. On the back are the dorsal fins. Pectoral fins are on the lower sides near the front, and pelvic fins are on the lower sides near the tail. The anal fin is on the underside just in front of the tail. The tail itself is called the caudal fin.

▲ A shark's dorsal (back) fin stops its whole body swinging from side to side while swimming.

SHARKS

304 Some sharks have tails longer than their bodies. The common thresher shark is 20 feet long—and half of this is its tail. The thresher uses it to attack smaller fish, so it can eat them.

▼ The thresher shark thrashes its tail from side to side to stun small fish before swallowing them.

QUIZ

1. How many pairs of gills do most sharks have— 5, 10, or 12?
2. Where are a shark's dorsal fins?
3. What do gills take in from water?

Answers:
1. 5 (10 gills) 2. On its back 3. Oxygen

305 Shark tails have other uses, too. Some sharks smack the water's surface with their tails to frighten their prey. Others swish away sand or mud on the seabed to reveal any hidden creatures.

BREATHING UNDERWATER
1. Most sharks have five pairs of gills.
2. Fine blood vessels allow oxygen to pass from the water to the blood.
3. Heart pumps blood around the body.

▶ A shark's gill chambers are in its neck region. Most have five gill slits on either side.

306 Like other fish, sharks breathe underwater using their gills. These are under the slits on either side of the head, and are filled with blood. Water flows in through the shark's mouth, over the gills, and out through the slits. The gills take in oxygen from the water because sharks need oxygen to survive.

307 Most sharks swim all of the time so that water flows over their gills and they can breathe. However some can lie still and make the water flow over their gills by "pumping" the muscles of their mouth and neck.

127

Shark bodies

308 A shark has a skeleton but it is different to ours. The parts are made not of bone, but of a substance called cartilage. This substance is very strong and light, and also slightly bendy.

QUIZ
Which of the following organs do both humans and sharks have in their bodies?
1. Stomach 2. Lungs
3. Spiral valve 4. Liver
5. Gills 6. Heart

Answers: 1, 4, 6

309 A shark's guts are about twice as long as its body. Swallowed food goes into the stomach, then along the intestine. This has a part called a spiral valve, found only in sharks and rays. It is shaped like a corkscrew and takes in nutrients from food.

Dorsal fin

Kidney

Intestines have a spiral valve

Backbone extends into tail

Stomach

310 Many sharks produce slime from their skin. It slides off the shark easily and helps the shark to swim faster. New slime is always being made quickly by the skin to replace the slime that flows away.

▲ The main parts of the skeleton are the skull, the ribs, the long backbone or vertebral column, and the fin spines.

SHARKS

311 Sharks have very tough skin covered with tiny, tooth-shaped points. These points are called denticles. In the bramble shark some of the denticles are much larger, forming sharp thorns and prickles for protection.

312 Shark skin can be useful. Through the ages it has been used by people as a strong material to make handbags, shoes, belts, cases, handle grips, and even a special kind of sandpaper known as chagrin.

▲▶ An enlarged view of the swell shark's skin shows the tiny toothlike scales, called denticles.

Ultimate Killer

313 The world's biggest hunting, or predatory, fish is the great white shark. It grows to 20 feet in length and can weigh more than one ton. Great whites live around the world, mainly in warmer seas. They have a fearsome reputation.

▼ When attacking, the great white's final upward rush, or charge, can carry it up to 16 feet above the surface.

314 The great white can raise its body temperature. It can make its body warmer than the surrounding water. This allows its muscles to work more quickly, so it can swim powerfully. It means the great white is partly warm-blooded, like humans.

315 Great whites let their victims bleed to death. They bite on their first charge then move off, leaving the victim with terrible wounds. When the injured prey is weak, the great white comes back to finish it off.

I DON'T BELIEVE IT!
A great white has about 300 razor-sharp teeth in its mouth. Its jaws open wide enough to swallow a whole seal in one gulp!

SHARKS

316 **The teeth of the great white are up to 2 inches long.** They are razor-sharp but slim, like blades, and they sometimes snap off. But new teeth are always growing just behind, ready to move forward and replace the snapped-off teeth.

▼ The great white's upper teeth are triangular, the lower ones more pointed.

▼ Each tooth has jagged, sawlike edges called serrations.

317 **The great white "saws" lumps from its victim.** Each tooth has tiny sharp points along its edges. As the shark starts to feed, it bites hard and then shakes its head from side to side. The teeth work like rows of small saws to slice off a mouthful.

318 **The great white often attacks unseen from below.** It surges up from the dark depths with tremendous power. It can smash into big prey such as a seal or a dolphin, and lift it right out of the water as it takes its first bite.

▶ When chasing prey or bait, great whites reach a top speed of over 25 miles an hour.

Strange sharks

319 **Six-gill sharks have an extra pair of gills.** This may be the number that ancient sharks had long ago. Six-gill sharks grow up to 16 feet long and eat various foods, from shellfish to dead dolphins.

Six pairs of curled gill slits

320 **Some sharks have frills.** The frilled shark has six pairs of wavy gill slits. It looks more like an eel than a shark, with a slim body 6.5 feet in length, and long frilly fins. It is dark brown in color, lives in very deep waters, and eats squid and octopus.

▲ Each tooth of the frilled shark has three needlelike points for grabbing soft-bodied prey.

▼ A saw shark may lose and regrow as many as 30,000 teeth during its lifetime.

321 **The saw shark has a "saw" for a nose.** Its long nose, or snout, is up to half its total length. The snout has teethlike points sticking out from the sides. The shark uses its snout to dig around in sand and mud for prey.

322 **The goblin shark looks very strange!** Few examples have been found, so little is known about its lifestyle. It swims in very deep waters where there is no light—it may be able to detect its prey using an electro-sense.

▲ This young goblin shark has not yet grown its extra-long nose.

▼ The adult goblin shark's snout can be one-quarter of its total length. The jaws can move forward, out of the mouth, to grab small fish and squid.

I DON'T BELIEVE IT!
The smallest sharks could lie curled up in your hand. The dwarf lanternshark is just 8 inches long!

323 **Lanternsharks can glow in the dark!** They live in deep dark water and have glowing spots on their bodies, particularly around their mouths and along their sides. The spots may attract curious small creatures such as fish and squid, so the shark can snap them up.

▶ The lanternshark's tiny light-producing organs are called photophores.

Amazing senses

324 Most sharks have big eyes and can see well in the dark ocean. Many feed at night, or in deeper water where there's little light. This makes eyesight very important to the shark so that it can spot its prey. Some sharks have eyes that glow in the dark.

▲ A porbeagle shark uses its keen eyesight to chase its favorite food—mackerel.

▼ A tiger shark's eye has membrane to protect it from injury caused by struggling prey.

325 Sharks can detect electricity. As sea animals move, their muscles give off tiny pulses of electricity into the water. A shark has hundreds of tiny pits over its snout called ampullae of Lorenzini. These detect the electric pulses. A shark can even sense prey buried out of sight in mud.

I DON'T BELIEVE IT!
The blind shark of Australia can see, but not very well. When it's caught, it closes its eyes so tightly that it appears to have none!

Each ampulla looks like a tiny hole in the shark's snout.

326
Sharks can hear divers breathing! They detect the sound of air bubbles coming from the scuba divers' mouths. Hearing is not a shark's best sense—its ear openings are tiny.

▼ Sharks detect a diver by sight, sound and feeling ripples—the dive suit reduces smell and electro-sensing.

327
Sharks have an amazing sense of smell. It is their best long-range sense. From several kilometres away, they can detect blood or body fluids from a wounded animal. A shark 'sniffs' water into the nostrils on its snout, just like a human draws air into his or her nose.

328
Sharks often test-taste their food before eating. They will take a small nibble of an unfamiliar food to check that it's suitable to eat. Some sharks have taste buds on their snouts, so they can detect the flavor of food by rubbing their noses on it.

329
Like us, sharks can feel things that touch their skin. They also have an extra sense organ called the lateral line. This is a long tube running down each side of a shark's body, under its skin. Ripples in the water pass into the lateral line through tiny holes in the skin. Hairs inside the lateral line sense the ripples and send signals to the brain.

◀ The lateral line runs along the side of the body from head to tail base.

Lateral line

Hide and seek

330 Some sharks blend into their surroundings. This is called camouflage. The wobbegong has a lumpy body with blotches and frills that look just like rocks and seaweed. It waits for a fish to swim past, then opens its huge mouth to grab the victim.

▶ The mottled pattern, lumpy skin, and frilly mouth of the wobbegong means it is difficult to spot from above, as it lies silently on the seabed.

331 A young zebra shark's stripes may camouflage it as it lies on ridges of mud or sand formed by water currents. The stripes also blend in with the shadows on the seabed formed by ripples on the surface above. As the shark grows, its stripes split into spots.

▼ This adult zebra shark's spots were once connected to form stripes.

SHARKS

▲ The flattened body of the angel shark looks like a low hump or rise in the sandy seabed. The shark must stay still to make the most of its camouflage.

332 **Angel sharks have wide, flat bodies the same color as sand.** They blend perfectly into the sandy seabed as they lie in wait for prey. They are called "angel" sharks because their fins spread wide like an angel's wings.

333 **Even in the open ocean, sharks can be hard to spot.** This is because of the way they are colored, known as countershading. The shark's back is darker while its underside is lighter. Seen from above the dark back blends in with the gloom of deeper water below. Seen from below, the pale belly merges with the brighter water's surface and sky above.

TRUE OR FALSE?

1. Angel sharks have brightly colored bodies.
2. Sharks have dark bellies and pale backs.
3. Zebra sharks can be spotty.

Answers:
1. False 2. False, they are dark on top and light below 3. True, an adult zebra shark has spots

▲ A side view of this gray reef shark shows countershading—a darker back and a lighter underside.

137

Save our sharks

QUIZ
Put these sharks in order of size, starting with the smallest to the biggest:
A. Great white
B. Lesser spotted dogfish
C. Nurse shark
D. Frilled shark

Answers:
1. B 2. D 3. C 4. A

334 Some shark species have become very rare. There are lots of reasons for this—pollution, hunting by people who think that all sharks are dangerous, sports angling where people use rods and lines to hook sharks, catching sharks for their meat, and catching sharks by accident in nets meant for other fish.

▼ By getting very close to sharks, and studying their behavior, experts can help the conservation effort.

◄ Disguarded fishing nets can trap sharks, such as this young hammerhead.

335 Live sharks can be worth more than dead ones. People pay to see sharks in their natural habitats, viewing from glass-bottomed boats or underwater tunnels. In ecotourism, people experience nature without damaging it, and profits are used to help animals, plants, and their habitats.

336 Sadly, sharks can be made into many foods, including shark fin soup. Many other shark parts are eaten or used by people around the world, including the flesh as shark steaks, and the liver and other body parts in various oils, cosmetics, and health foods. Sometimes, it's not obvious because names are changed. Meat from a dogfish shark may be sold as "rock salmon" or "rock cod."

▲ Shark oil is said to improve health, but there is no scientific proof.

337 Some sharks need our help, or they will die out forever. One of the best ways is to set aside huge areas of sea and coast as marine nature reserves or sanctuaries. Here all the animals can be protected from harm.

WHALES AND DOLPHINS

338 Whales, dolphins, and porpoises are a fascinating group of marine animals also known as cetaceans. Like other members of the mammal animal group, they have warm blood and breathe air. Almost all kinds live in the sea, apart from a few species of dolphin that live in freshwater rivers and lakes. This intelligent group holds many records—the biggest animal in the world, the largest hunter, and some of the fastest, deepest-diving creatures ever to have lived.

▶ Many kinds of dolphin live in groups called schools. Common dolphins are colorful, with yellow or tan patches along their sides and dark "spectacles" around their eyes.

The greatest animals

339 Whales are the biggest kind of animal alive today. Some are longer and heavier than the largest trucks. They need lots of muscle power and energy to move their large bodies. As they live in the ocean, the water helps to support their huge bulk.

340 The blue whale is the largest animal ever. It can grow up to 100 feet in length, which is as long as seven cars placed end to end. It reaches up to 165 tons in weight—that's as heavy as 35 elephants.

▶ The blue whale is a true giant, as large as a submarine. Yet it is also gentle and swims slowly, unless frightened or injured.

WHALES AND DOLPHINS

341 On land, bears and tigers are the biggest hunting animals. However, the sperm whale is more than 100 times larger, making it the biggest predator (active hunter) on Earth. It grows up to 65 feet in length and 55 tons in weight.

TRUE OR FALSE?
1. The sperm whale is the biggest predator.
2. The blue whale weighs up to 30 tons in weight.
3. Whales breathe oxygen through gills.

Answers:
1. True 2. False, it can weigh up to 150 tons 3. False

342 The animal with the largest mouth is the bowhead whale. Its body is 60 feet long, and its mouth makes up almost one-third of its length. Fin whales are the second largest whales, at an impressive 85 feet long.

▼ Killer whales come to the surface and open their nostrils, called blowholes, to breathe. They then dive back into the water again. The blowholes stay closed underwater.

343 Whales breathe air, just like humans. They must hold their breath as they dive underwater to feed. A few of them, such as the bottlenose whale, can stay underwater for more than one hour. Most humans have trouble holding their breath for even one minute!

▶ Bottlenose dolphins swim underwater for long periods of time, searching for food. They must then return to the surface to take in oxygen.

One big family

MAKE A DOLPHIN!
You will need:
paper   colored pens or pencils
Draw a dolphin outline and color it any pattern you like. You can name it after its color, such as the pink-spotted dolphin. Or use your own name, like Claire's dolphin.

344 The mammal group of cetaceans is made up of about 80 kinds of whale, dolphin, and porpoise. The whale group is then divided into two main types—baleen whales and toothed whales.

▼ The sperm whale is the biggest of the toothed whales. It only seems to have teeth in its lower jaw because those in its upper jaw can barely be seen.

345 Baleen whales are the largest members of the cetacean group. They are often called great whales. The sei whale, for example, is about 50 feet long. Baleen whales catch food with long strips in their mouths called baleen, or whalebone.

346 Toothed whales catch prey with their sharp teeth. This subgroup includes sperm whales, beaked whales, and pilot whales. One example is the beluga, or white whale. It is one of the noisiest whales, making clicks, squeaks, and trills.

◄ The beluga lives in the cold waters of the Arctic and can grow up to 16 feet in length.

WHALES AND DOLPHINS

▼ The finless porpoise, with its blunt "beak" and bulging forehead, is one of the smallest cetaceans at about 5 feet in length.

348 Another group is made up of beaked whales. These are medium-sized whales with long, beak-shaped mouths. There are about 20 kinds, but some are very rare and hardly ever seen. The shepherd's beaked whale, which is about 23 feet in length, has been seen fewer than 20 times.

347 There are six species of porpoise. They are usually quite small, at 6.5 feet or less in length. They have blunter, more rounded heads than dolphins. The finless porpoise, as its name suggests, has a smooth back with no fin.

Gray patch from eye to the flipper

Back is a dusky blue-black color

▶ The dusky dolphin is very inquisitive and likes to swim and leap near boats, perhaps in the hope of being fed.

White underside

349 There are more than 35 kinds of dolphin. Most of them are 6 to 10 feet in length. They are fast swimmers and can often be seen leaping above the waves. The dusky dolphin is one of the highest leapers, twisting and somersaulting before it splashes back into the sea.

Inside whales and dolphins

350 Whales, dolphins, and porpoises are mammals. They have the same parts inside their bodies as humans. These include bones to make up the skeleton, lots of muscles, a stomach to hold food, a heart to pump blood, and lungs to breathe air.

351 Most mammals have hair or fur. Whales, dolphins, and porpoises are unusual because they have smooth, hairless skin to make them streamlined. Only a few hairs, mainly bristles, can be found around the eyes, nose, and mouth.

◀ Most of the inner parts of a dolphin and human are alike. They are also in similar positions inside the body.

352 On land, fur keeps mammals warm in cold places. The sea can be cold, too. Cetaceans have a different way of keeping in their body heat. They have a thick layer of fat just under the skin called blubber. In large whales, the blubber can be more than 20 inches thick!

▼ Blubber is the layer of fat underneath the skin of whales, dolphins, and porpoises. It is about five times thicker than the layer of fat beneath human skin.

50–54 vertebrae (backbones), but no bones in the tail flukes.

Skull

Barrel-shaped rib cage

Flipper bone

Powerful jaws

Strong teeth

▲ The skeleton of a whale or dolphin, such as this killer whale, is made up of bones. There are no rear leg bones and no bones in the dorsal fin (on the back) or in the tail flukes.

Fluke

353 Compared to most animals, whales, dolphins, and porpoises have large brains for their size. Dolphins are clever creatures, able to learn tricks and solve simple puzzles. Some scientists believe that dolphins have even developed their own way of communicating.

354 Cetaceans often have small animals growing inside their bodies called parasites, such as lice. Parasites aren't needed for survival—the whale or dolphin provides them with food. Some baleen whales have their heads covered with barnacles (shellfish), which normally grow on seaside rocks.

▲ Barnacles are a type of shellfish. They stick firmly to large whales and cannot be rubbed off!

I DON'T BELIEVE IT!

The sperm whale has the biggest brain in the world. It weighs about 18 pounds—that's over five times the size of a human brain. But its large brain does not mean it is the cleverest animal.

Flippers, flukes, and fins

355 **Most mammals have four legs and a tail.** Instead, whales, dolphins, and porpoises have flippers, a fin, and a tail. Flippers are their front limbs, similar to human arms. In fact, flipper bones and human arm and hand bones are alike. Flippers are mainly used for swimming, scratching, and waving to send messages to others in the group.

356 **The tail of a cetacean is in two almost identical parts.** Each part is called a fluke. Unlike the flippers, flukes have no bones. They are used for swimming as the body arches powerfully to swish them up and down. They can also be slapped onto the water's surface to send messages to other whales. This is called lobtailing.

▼ Whales can often be seen splashing backward into the water. This is known as breaching. Even the huge humpback whale can breach—and it weighs more than 33 tons!

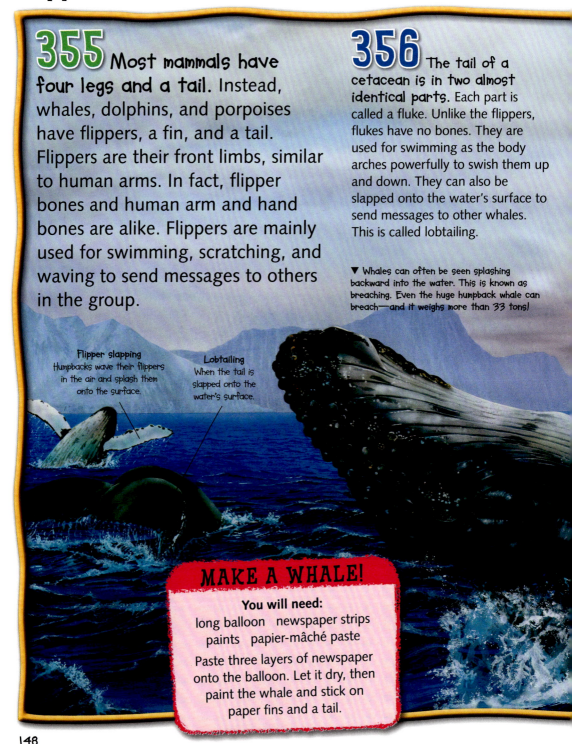

Flipper slapping
Humpbacks wave their flippers in the air and splash them onto the surface.

Lobtailing
When the tail is slapped onto the water's surface.

MAKE A WHALE!

You will need:
long balloon   newspaper strips
paints   papier-mâché paste

Paste three layers of newspaper onto the balloon. Let it dry, then paint the whale and stick on paper fins and a tail.

WHALES AND DOLPHINS

357 Many whales, dolphins, and porpoises jump out of the water. They then crash back down again with a big splash—this is called breaching. It may be done to send a loud message to others in the group, or to try and get rid of skin pests, such as barnacles and whale lice.

358 The fin on the back of many whales, dolphins and porpoises is known as a dorsal fin. In some, such as the killer whale, it is tall and narrow. In others, such as the bottlenose dolphin, it is shaped like a swept-back triangle. Blue whales have a tiny dorsal fin near the tail. Right whales, bowheads, belugas, and narwhals have no dorsal fin at all.

Blue whale

Killer whale

Bottlenose dolphin

▲ Many whales, dolphins, and porpoises can be recognized by their distinctive dorsal fin shapes.

Sensitive senses

359 Whales, dolphins, and porpoises have many of the same senses as humans. Like us, they use sight and hearing, but because they live underwater these senses detect very different surroundings. A whale's eyes have adapted to cope with underwater conditions far better than a human's.

▼ Atlantic spotted dolphins roll over and rub each other. It's like saying, "Hello, we're in the same school."

360 One sense that humans don't have, but whales, dolphins, and porpoises do is the ability to detect magnetism. Some whales may "feel" the Earth's weak magnetic force, which humans would detect using a compass. This magnetic sense may help them to find their way on their long journeys, or migrations, through the wide and featureless ocean.

361 Whales, dolphins, and porpoises have very sensitive skin, so the sense of touch is important to them. They rub and stroke others in their group, or a partner during breeding time. A mother whale often caresses her baby to provide comfort and warmth.

QUIZ
1. Do dolphins have a strong sense of taste?
2. Cetaceans use what word beginning with "e" to sense objects?
3. Which sense do some whales use when migrating?

Answers:
1. No, it is very weak 2. Echolocation 3. Magnetic sense

WHALES AND DOLPHINS

362 Dolphins have a weak sense of smell, if any at all. Instead, they use their strong sense of taste to tell them about the foods they are eating. They can also taste the water. This lets them know what other bits of food might be drifting nearby.

363 Hearing is vital for whales, dolphins, and porpoises. They don't have outer ears, like us. Instead, sounds in the water are detected inside the head. Many toothed whales find their way in dark water by making clicking sounds, then listening to the echoes that bounce off nearby objects. This method is called echolocation.

▶ Killer whales spyhop—look across the surface of the water—for the fins of others in their group or for signs of enemies, such as sharks.

Clicks, squeaks, and squeals

364 Whales, dolphins, and porpoises can be very noisy animals. They make loud clicks and whistles to help them navigate, hunt prey, and communicate with each other. These noises travel long distances underwater, so divers can often hear them. Some whale noises can be heard more than 60 miles away.

▼ During echolocation, dolphins create high-pitched clicks in their nasal passages by pushing air between phonic lips. This action causes vibrations and sound waves to form.

365 Sounds are especially important for detecting objects by echolocation. The dolphin detects the returning echoes of its own clicks. It can then work out the size and shape of objects nearby—whether a rock, coral, a shipwreck, or a shoal of fish.

Brain
Air sacs
Blow hole
Phonic lips
Clicks pass through the melon.
Sound waves from the dolphin.
Sound waves returning from the fish.
Returning echoes are detected by fat-filled sinuses in the lower jaw.
Inner ear

366 The sounds are made by air moving around inside the animal's breathing passages. In dolphins, sound waves are brought together, or focused, by the large fluid-filled lump inside the forehead called the melon. This makes sounds travel out from the front of the head in a narrow beam.

WHALES AND DOLPHINS

367 **Sounds are also used for communication.** Belugas and dolphins especially make a vast range of clicks, squeals, and squeaks. Sounds help them to stay together in their groups, and to work together when hunting fish.

◀ Scientists think that dolphins may use sound to identify other members of their pod.

◀ This whale is about to slap the surface of the water with its fluke. This is one way whales make noises with their bodies to talk to each other.

368 **Scientists have spent time closely watching dolphins to see if they use a language to communicate.** Certain sounds seem to occur more often when dolphins are resting, swimming, playing, feeding, or breeding.

MAKE DOLPHIN NOISES

You will need:
sheet of paper   ruler   plastic comb

Roll the paper into a funnel and squeal through the narrow end. Rub the teeth of the comb along a ruler to produce dolphinlike clicks.

Long-distance swimmers

▲ Baleen whales, such as the humpback, make long journeys so that they can give birth in tropical waters. Then the baby is able to grow stronger in calm waters before migrating to colder areas.

369 **Many cetaceans migrate (go on long journeys) to find food at the same time each year.** Baleen whales spend summer in cold northern or southern waters where there are vast amounts of food. For winter they swim back to the tropics. Although there is little food there, the water is warm and calm.

370 **Baleen whales usually swim in groups as they migrate.** They can often be seen "spyhopping." This means they swing around into an upright position, lift their heads above the water and turn slowly to look all around as they sink back into the water. This is especially common in whales that migrate along coasts.

I DON'T BELIEVE IT!
The migration of the gray whale takes less than six weeks. It would take a strong swimmer 30 weeks to complete the same journey.

371 **The gray whale makes the longest migration of any whale—and mammal.** In spring, gray whales swim from their breeding areas in the subtropical waters around the coast of Mexico. They head north along the west coast of North America to the Arctic Ocean for summer feeding. In fall, they return in the opposite direction.

In summer, gray whales swim back to the coast of Alaska to feed.

In winter, the whales travel south to Mexico to have babies.

▲ Gray whales travel up to 12,500 miles every year, between the icy Arctic region and warm subtropical waters.

372 **Belugas and narwhals migrate from the cold waters of the southern area of the Arctic Ocean to the even icier waters further north!** They follow the edge of the ice sheet as it shrinks and melts back each spring, then grows again each fall.

◀ This conservation worker is fitting a satellite transmitter to a beluga whale to keep track of its movements as it migrates.

373 **Many cetaceans can now be tracked by satellite.** A radio beacon is fixed, usually to the dorsal fin, and its signals are picked up by satellites in space. This shows that some whales complete exactly the same migration every year, while others wander far more widely around the oceans.

Index

Entries in **bold** refer to main subject entries. Entries in *italics* refer to illustrations.

A

abyssal plains 20, *20*, 27
Abyssal Zone *8*, *18*, **20–21**, *20*, 22
algae 48, 64, 71, 80, *80*
amphipods *9*, 25, 26, *26*
anemones *30*, 32, *32*, 46, *46*, *48*, *52*, 67, 69, 70, *70*, *91*, 107, *107*, **113**
anglerfish *9*, **40–41**, *40*, *41*
Antarctic Ocean 27
arches 92, *92*
Arctic Ocean *8*, 28, 19
artificial reefs 82, *82*
Atlantic Ocean *8*, 28, 31, 53, 59, 62
atolls 54, 55, *55*, *105*
Australia 60, 69, *69*

B

bacteria *27*, 29, 31, *38*, 40
barnacles *91*, 107
barracudas 57, *57*
barrier reefs 54, *54*, 56, *56*
basket stars 58
bats 111
bays 93, *93*
beaches 86, 91, 92–93, *93*, 98–99, *98–99*, *102*, *104*, 108, *108*, 109, *109*, 117, *118–119*, 119
bioluminescence **36–37**, *36*
birds 95, 96, *96*, 97, 99, 101, 109, **110–111**, *110*, *111*, 122
black mangroves *100*
black smokers 28, *28*
blacktip reef sharks 77, *105*
blue-ringed octopus 69, *69*
blue-spotted stingray *52*
blue tang fish *66*
bobtail squid 65, *65*
Bondi Beach *118–119*
bottlenose dolphins 57, 62, *62*
box jellyfish 69, *69*, 77
boxer crabs 70
brain corals 50, *51*, 56
breathing 12, 14, **34**, *34*, 35
bull sharks 68
buoyancy 10, 35
butterflies 111, *111*
butterfly fish 45, *45*, *57*, 78, *78*

C

camouflage 66
carbon dioxide 12, 30
Caribbean reef octopus 53, *53*
Caribbean Sea 53, *53*, **62–63**, 78
caves 92, *93*
chalk 89, *89*
clams 97, *97*, 98, 113
cleaner wrasses 71, *71*
cliffs 86, *88*, 89, 92, *93*, 110, *110*, 111
climate change **123**
clownfish 70, *70*
coastal flood defenses 123
cockles 97, *97*, 113, 116
cold seeps 31
cold water reefs **58–59**, *58*
colonies 46, 49, *49*, 51
color 46, 50, **66–67**, *66*, *67*, 78
comb jellies 15, *15*, *33*
cone shells 68, *68*
continental shelf **8**, 12, *20*
Cook, James 60
copepods 26, *33*, 38
coral *9*, *13*
  bleaching **80–81**, *80*
  reefs **30–31**, *30*, *31*, *94*, *105*
  reproduction 49, 50
Coral Sea 53, 60, 61
Coral Triangle 52
coral trout 66
cordgrass 96, 97
crabeater seals 94
crabs 6, *27*, *28*, 31, 47, 52, *52*, 71, *71*, 94, 99, *99*, 101, 107, 108, 111, **112**, *112*, 116, 122
crown-of-thorns starfish 79, *79*
crustaceans 19, 38
cup corals 48, *48*
currents **10**, *10*, 32, 38, 86, 88, 91, *92*, *93*, 98, 100, 102, *103*, *104*, 106
cuttlefish 66

D

damselfish 52, *52*
Dark Zone *8*, **18–19**, 33, 39
Darwin, Charles 54
D-Day 117, *117*
deep sea reefs 58, 59
deltas *93*, 104
density **10**, *10*
divers 68, 73, **76–77**, *76*, *77*
diving **34**, *35*
dolphins 52, 57, 62, *62*
dugongs 52, 60, *60*
dunes *93*, **99**, *99*, 111

E

Earth 90, *90*, 94, 123
earthquakes 89, 114, *114*
ecosystems 8, 31, 38, 46, 47, 63, 65, 74, 79, 80, 81, 82, *82*, 83
eels *9*, *39*, 43
elkhorn coral *50*, 55, *56*
Endeavour, HMS 60
energy 9, 12, 31, 32, 34, 38
erosion **88**, *88*, 89, *92*, 95
estuaries 93, 96, **104–105**, *104*, 123

F
fangtooth fish 9, **18**, *18*, 39
feather stars 56
fire coral *115*
fish 94, 95, 98, 99, *99*, 101, 107, 108, 111, **112**, 113, 116, *116*, 122
fishing 55, 59, 61, 63, *74*, 79, 81, 82, 83, 116, *116*, 119, 123, *123*
flamingos 105
flashlight fish 73, *73*
Florida Keys National Marine Sanctuary 46, *46*
food chains and webs 13, **38–39**
freshwater 96, *96*, 104
fringing reefs 54, *54*

G
giant clams 53, *53*, 71
giant isopods **19**, *19*
giant squid **16–17**, *16*
glasswort 96, *96*
global conveyor *10*
global warming 80, 83, **123**
goblin shark **39**, *39*
Goliath grouper *76*
goose barnacles *113*
gopher rockfish *46*
granite 89, *89*
Great Barrier Reef 53, **60–61**, *60*, *74*, *75*, 78
green turtles *109*, *123*
Greenland sharks **19**, *19*, 26
grizzly bears *104*
groynes 91, *92*
gulper eel 9, **39**, *39*

H
habitats 84, 86, 90, 100, 102, 104, 107, 123

Hadal Zone 8, **24–25**
hagfish 9, **21**, *21*, 26
hard-bodied corals **50–51**
hatchet fish 9, **36**, *43*, *43*
Hawaii 53, **64–65**, *65*
headlands 92, *92*
hermit crabs 71, *71*, 91, *107*, *112*
high tides 90, *90*, 91, 97, 98, 99, 103, *103*
humpback whales 64, *64*, 65
Humuhumunukunu-kuapua'a fish 53, *53*
hydrothermal vents 6, **28–29**, *29*

I
ice 94, *94*
Indian Ocean 8, 28, 52, 53, 55, 78
insects 96, **111**

J
jellyfish 48, 69, *69*, 77, 98, 115

K
Komodo National Park 83, *83*
krill 38

L
lagoons 103, **104–105**, *105*
lantern fish **33**, *33*, 37
lava 65, *65*, 89, *89*
leafy seadragons 60, *60*
leisure **118–119**
lemon sharks 68, *68*, 101
lettuce corals 51, *57*
light 8, 42, 43
  bioluminescence **36–37**, *36*
Light Zone 8, 9, **12–13**, 33, *33*, 38, *38*
lighthouses **115**, *115*

limpets 91, 107, *107*, 116, *121*
lionfish 67, *67*
lobsters 72
longshore drift **91**, *92*
lophelia coral 58
low tides 90, *90*, 97, 106

M
Maldives 55
mandarin fish 73, *73*
mangrove swamps **100–101**, *101*
mangrove trees 47, *47*, 62, 100, *100*
mantis shrimps 69
Mariana Trench **24**, *24*, 25
marine snow **18**, 20, 26, *38*
maze coral *57*
Mesoamerican Reef 62, *62*
Mid-Atlantic Ridge 28
migration *109*, *109*
Moon 90, *90*
moray eels 71, *71*
mountains 9, *20*
mudflats 93, *93*, **96–97**, 103
mudskippers *112*
mushroom coral *51*
mussels 91, 107, *107*, *111*, 113, 116

N
natural disasters **114**
nautilus **14**, *14*
neap tides **90**, *90*
nests 110, *110*
nocturnal animals **72–73**, *72*
nutrients 20, 29, 38, *38*

O
octopuses 53, 69, *69*, 72, 77
oil 120, 121, 122
olive sea snakes 61, *61*

157

ooze **26**
otters 99, *99*, 108
owls 110
oxygen 11, 12, 13, 34, 35
oysters 113

P
Pacific Ocean 8, 24, 28, 53, 64, 65
panda butterflyfish 45, *45*
parrotfish 78, *78*
pebbles *88*, *92*, **102–103**, *102*, 112
photophores 36, *36*, 37, 39, 41, *43*
photosynthesis 12
phytoplankton **13**, *33*, 38, *38*
plankton 9, 11, 13
planulas 49, *49*, 65
plate coral *56*
pleasure piers **119**, *119*
pollution 30, 59, *80*, 81, 83, **122**, *122–123*
polyps 46, 47, **48–49**, *48*, *49*, 50, *50*, 51, 52, 53, 55, 56, 59, 64, 65, 70, 71, 72, 74, 77, 78, *78*, 79, 80, *80*, 81
porcelain crabs 52, *52*
ports *120–121*
power stations 120
predators 66, 67, *67*, **68–69**, 70, 76
prey 66, **68–69**, *68*, 73
proboscis monkey 101, *101*

Q
queen angelfish 62, *62*

R
rattails 9, **21**, *21*, 26, *26*
Red Sea 52
red soldierfish 73, *73*
regal angelfish 66
remora fish 70, *70*, 71

ringed plovers 103, *103*
rivers 93, *93*, 96, 104, *104*, 116
rock pools **107**, *107*
rocks 85, 86, 88, *88*, 89, 92, 102, 106, 107, 108, *111*, 115
rocky shores *91*, **106–107**

S
saltmarshes 93, *93*, **96–97**, *96–97*
salty water 86, 87, 96, 97, 104, 114, *114*
sand 86, *88*, 89, 91, 93, 97, 98, *98*, 99, *99*, 102, *109*, 111, 118, *118*
sandy beaches 84, *93*, **98–99**, *98–99*, 103
scallops 98, 113, *113*, 116
scavengers 20, *21*, 26, 38
scuba diving 118, *118*
sea anemones 46, 48, 52, *52*, 67, 69, 70, *70*
sea asters 96, *96*
seabed 95, *98*, 114, 123
sea cucumbers 9, 21, **27**, *38*, 47
sea fans *51*, 57, *57*
sea goldies 57
sea grasses 7, 55, 56, *56*
sea holly *111*
sea kale 102, *103*
sea lions 108, *108*
sea mounts 20, *20*
sea slugs 67, *67*
sea snails 59, 68, *68*
sea snakes 61, *61*, 77
sea sponges 58
sea thrift 96, *96*
sea turtles 109, 122
sea urchins 56, 79
sea walls 117, 119, 123, *123*
sea whips *51*, 57
seahorses 53, *53*

seals 108, 122
seaweeds 64, 68, 74, 79, 85, 91, 94, **106**, *106*, 107, 111, 112, 116
sediments 89, 91, 92, *92*, 93, 96, 104
sharks *11*, 13, **19**, *19*, 26, *33*, 34, 39, 57, *57*, 63, *63*, 59, 68, *68*, 71, 75, 77, *101*, *105*, 116
shelled animals 97, *97*
shellfish 96, *104*, 105, 107, **113**, 115, 116
shells 97, *112*, 113, 116
shingle *92*, **102–103**, *102*, 105
shingle spits *92*, **103**, *103*
silversidefish 48
"Skeleton Coast" 122
snipe eel **43**, *43*
soft tree corals *47*, *51*
soft-bodied corals 47, *47*, 49, **50–51**
soft-shell clams 97
Southern elephant seal *108*
Southern Ocean *8*, 51
sperm whales **14**, *14*, 16, 17, *33*, **35**, *35*
spiny lobsters 72
spireshells 97, *97*
spits 93
sponges **22–23**, *22*, *23*, 47, 57, 59, 79
spring tides **90**, *90*, 93, 96
squid 6, 9, 14, *33*, 35, 37, 42, *42*, 65, 66
stacks 85, 92, *92*
staghorn coral 50, *50*, 57
star coral 57
starfish 56, 79, *79*, 85, 91, 94, 107, *107*, **113**, *113*
stingrays 52, *52*, 56, 63, 73
stonefish 115, *115*
storms 95, *95*, 97, 102, *102*, 103, *104*, 121, *122*, 123

158

strandlines 99, *99*, 103
submarines 25
submersibles *21*
Sun 90, *90*, 107, 118
sunlight **9**, *9*, **12**
sweetlips fish 61, *61*
symbiosis **70–71**

T

temperature **11**, 28
terns *109*
threadfin butterfly fish 78, *78*
tidal bulge *90*
tidal pools *85*
tidal zones **91**, *91*, 106, 107
tides 86, 88, **90–91**, *90*, 98, *98*, 104, 107, 113, *116*, 121
tourism 55, 63, 75, *75*, 81, 83, *117*, 118–119, 122
towershells 97, *97*
trade 116, 117, **120–121**, *120–121*
trenches 9, 20, *20*, **24**
Trieste submarine **25**, *25*
tripod fish **27**, *27*
tsunamis 114, *114*
tube worms *8*, **29**, *29*
turtles *56*, 65, *65*, 70, *70*, 71
Twilight Zone *8*, 13, **14–15**, 16, 33, 36, 43

U

urchins *56*, 79

V

Venus' flower basket 22, *22*, 23, *23*
vertical migration **33**, *33*
viperfish 9, 36, *36*
volcanoes 9, 20, *20*, 54, 64, 65, 89, 114

W

walruses 108
wave power 121, *121*
waves 86, 88, *88*, *89*, 91, 92, *92*, 93, *93*, 94, 95, 98, 100, 102, 105, 106, 114, *114*, 117, 118, 121
whale sharks 63, *63*
whales *34*, 35, 39, 52, 64, *64*, 65
 dead 26, *27*
 pilot **35**
 sperm **14**, *14*, 16, 17, *33*, **35**, *35*
whitetip reef sharks 57
winds 88, *88*, 91, 93, 95, 98, 99, 100, 102, 106, 114
wobbegong sharks 57
wolffish 59, *59*
worms 26, 27, *27*, 35, 59, 68, 72, *72*, 73

Z

zones **56–57**, *56*
zooplankton 13, 32, 38, *38*, 59, *59*
zooxanthellae 48, *49*, 52, 53, 70, 71, 78, 80, *80*, 81

Acknowledgments

The publishers would like to thank the following sources for the use of their photographs:
Key: t = top, b = bottom, l = left, r = right, c = center, bg = background

Front cover illustration Stuart Jackson Carter **Back cover** (l) Shutterstock/Joe Gough; (tc) Shutterstock/Yai; (tr) Shutterstock/Vlad61; (bc) Shutterstock/Matt9122; (br) Shutterstock/jarvis gray **Endpapers** Shutterstock/frantisekhojdysz

Alamy 40(tr) ©Walt Disney Co./Courtesy Everett Collection; 47(b) WaterFrame; 115(t) David Lyons; 116(b) Tibor Bognar; 138–139(bg) Reinhard Dirscherl; 58(bg) National Geographic/Uli Kunz

Ardea 22–23(bg) Pat Morris; 81(br) Kurt Amsler; 84–85 Bill Coster; 88(b) Mark Boulton; 94(t) Jean Paul Ferrero; 94(b) Valerie & Ron Taylor; 95(bg) John Daniels; 96–97(bg) David C Dixon; 102(bg) Mark Boulton; 104(bg) Jean Paul Ferrero; 104(br) M. Watson; 105(bg) Valerie & Ron Taylor; 106(b) Johan De Meester; 106(tr) Mark Boulton; 111(tl) Jean Paul Ferrero; 118–119(bg) Jean Paul Ferrero; 122–123(bg) Bob Gibbons; 122(tr) Thomas Dressler; 123(br) Duncan Usher; 103(bl) Dae Sasitorn

Dreamstime 52(bl) Roman Vintonyak; 52(c) Frhojdysz; 53(tr) Brento; 53(br) Andrew Jalbert; 66(cl) Olga Khoroshunova; 66(bl) Iliuta Goean; 72(br) John Anderson; 74(tr) Simon Gurney; 78(bl) Dirk Jan Mattaar; 78(tr) Stephankerkhofs; 127(cr) Naluphoto; 12 Tommy Schultz

FLPA 15(b) Fred Bavendam/Minden Pictures; 32(tr) Ingo Arndt/Minden Pictures; 32(bl) Norbert Wu/Minden Pictures; 39(br) Norbert Wu/Minden Pictures; 41(b) ImageBroker; 60(b) Mike Parry/Minden Pictures; 113(bg) D P Wilson; 115(br) Image Broker; 130–131(bg) Stephen Belcher/Minden Pictures; 138(bg) Biosphoto; Jeffrey Rotman/Biosphoto

Fotolia 12(cr) Tommy Schultz; 12(br) Desertdiver; 14–15(bg) & 24(tr) cornelius; 34(tr) zebra0209; 38(bl) cornelius; 53(bl) Iian Ben Tov; 55(br) Vladimir Ovchinnikov; 63(t) Peter Schinck; 67(tl) cbpix; 86(tr) Deborah Benbrook; 89(tr) Michael Siller; 100(bg) EcoView; 105(tr) Vladimir Ovchinnikov; 109(br) SLDigi; 118(tr) Ian Scott; 118(cl) Maribell

Getty 20(b) Corbis Documentary/Ralph White; 20(bl) Jean Tresfon; 36(r) Reinhard Dirscherl; 41(tr) Peter David; 46(br) Paul Kay; 54(b) Mint Images–Frans Lanting; 64(bg) Monica & Michael Sweet; 65(t) Dana Edmunds; 74(br) Wolfgang Poelzer; 76(bg) Jeff Hunter; 77(bg) Stephen Frink; 82(bg) Franco Banfi; 83(br) Auscape/Universal Images Group; 101(t) Brian J. Skerry/National Geographic; 114(b) Choo Youn-Kong; 120–121(bg) Bloomberg; 121(tr) Grant Duncan Smith

iStock 10(bg) Miguel Angelo Silva; 12(bl) tswinner; 34(tl) sethakan; 52(b) DaveBluck; 53(tl) andnyg; 61(br) tswinner; 63(bg) Allister Clark; 68–69(bg) NaluPhoto; 70–71(bg) TreasureGuard; 73(br) Olga Khoroshunova; 89(tl) shayes17; 112(tr) nealec; 117(bl) edgital; 119(br) igs942; 143(cl) sethakan

NASA 82–83(tc)

National Geographic 135(bg) Jim Abernathy

Nature Picture Library 48(bl) Jeff Rotman; 75(bg) Jurgen Freund; 79(t) Georgette Douwma

NOAA 10(cl) W H F Smith, NOAA; 24(cr) Archival Photography by Steve Nicklas, NOS, NGS; 29(tr) Pacific Ring of Fire 2004 Expedition. NOAA Office of Ocean Exploration; Dr. Bob Embley, NOAA PMEL, Chief Scientist; 31(tl) Image courtesy of Brooke et al, NOAA-OE, HBOI; 36(br) Image courtesy Edie Widder, NOAA

Nature Picture Library 23(br) Brandon Cole; 34(br) David Shale; 72–73(bg) Georgette Douwma; 124–125(bg) Doug Perrine; 137(t) Alex Mustard; 154(t) Tony Wu

Oceanwide Images 42(bg) & 61(tr) Gary Bell

Photoshot 155(bl) Tony Martin

Science Photo Library 6(bg) Dr Ken Macdonald; 44–45(bg) Georgette Douwma; 46(tr) Planetobserver; 80(bg) Georgette Douwma; 136(tr) Andy Murch/Visuals Unlimited, Inc.

Seapics 133(c) Hirose; 133(b) Espen Rekdal; 142(bg) Christopher Swann; 150–151(bg) Doug Perrine

Shutterstock 126(c) cbpix; 128–129(bg) Rich Carey; 129(tr) NatalieJean; 131(cl) BW Folsom; 131(br) cdelacy; 132–133(bg) Rich Carey; 133(tr) Sedin; 134(b) Greg Amptman; 135(b) cbpix; 136(b) Christophe Rouziou; 137(b) cbpix; 139(tr) Ru Bai Le; 143(b) Willyam Bradberry; 144(bg) Shane Gross; 144(bc) Shannon Workman; 146–147(bg) Menna; 147(br) Jan-Dirk Hansen; 149(tr) johan_R; 149(cr) Teo Dominguez; 149(br) Steve Noakes; 151(br) Ivan Cholakov; 153(tr) Sergey Popov V; 153(b) idreamphoto; 155(tr) maodoltee

All other photographs are from: DigitalSTOCK, digitalvision, John Foxx, PhotoAlto, PhotoDisc, PhotoEssentials, PhotoPro, Stockbyte

All artworks are from the Miles Kelly Artwork Bank

Every effort has been made to acknowledge the source and copyright holder of each picture.
Miles Kelly Publishing apologizes for any unintentional errors or omissions.